allabout
books

Here is an exciting introduction to five of the world's mightiest rivers—the Nile, the Amazon, the Yangtze, the Volga, and the Mississippi.

The story of a river is a thrilling tale of channels that change and shift, of crocodiles lurking in the swamps of the Nile, of howler monkeys screaming in the rain forest of the Amazon, of Chinese rivermen struggling to get their fragile boats through the dangerous rapids of the Yangtze.

With unusual narrative skill, Anne Terry White tells how these great rivers have developed through the ages—and how each one has affected the land and the people along its banks.

All About Great Rivers of the World

by Anne Terry White ■ illustrated by Kurt Wiese

RANDOM HOUSE
NEW YORK

TO SUSAN JOAN

This title was originally catalogued by the Library of Congress as follows:

White, Anne Terry.
 All about great rivers of the world; illustrated by Kurt
Wiese. New York, Random House ₁1957₎
  150 p. illus. 24 cm. (Allabout books, A–22)

  1. Rivers—Juvenile literature.   ɪ. Title.

PZ9.W5824A1   57—7520 ‡

Library of Congress   ₁68e²½₎

Trade Ed.: ISBN: 0-394-80222-5   Lib. Ed.: ISBN: 0-394-90222-X

Endpaper photograph from United Press International

Contents

1 The Call of the Rivers

In countless thousands, streams are flowing to the sea.

They roll through broad, flat valleys and narrow, mile-deep gorges, through tropical jungles and snowy wastes, through parkland and grassland, forest and desert, past farms and mills and towns. There is not one river too many; there is not one without a meaning for Man.

Long before he became a farmer, Man settled on the edge of streams. Rivers meant fresh water to drink, to

cook with, to bathe in. Rivers meant fish to catch, high-
ways to travel on. Man's boats and canoes went up the
rivers and down. How much easier and safer that was
than stumbling on foot through trackless forests where
fierce beasts lurked!

But something besides Man traveled on the surface of
the water—ideas went up and down the rivers with him.

"See what food and clothes and tools our neighbors
have," one village group said of another, gazing in wonder on the new.

"I'll give you this for that," they said.

And there was trade.

"See how those down-river people make pots, dry
fish. Look at their bows, their arrows and their snares.
See, they have tamed the wolf!"

And new arts were learned.

Progress moved along the rivers. It moved so fast that
the mountain people were for the most part left far
behind. Look at any map. You will see that most of
the great cities stand on rivers. These were once the
world's trade routes. London, Paris, New York, Cal-
cutta, Buenos Aires—all are river-route cities. See the
dots that stand for important towns. They, too, are
nearly always clustered near streams for the sake of

fertile land, of trade, of water power.

Man and his rivers are bound together inseparably. For a million years they have been shaping his life.

"Live here, not there," they said to him.

They told him: "Till the rich earth by our side."

They tempted him, saying: "Travel! See what lies beyond!"

They taught him: "There is profit in exchange."

They beckoned him: "Grind your corn; build your factories. Our water will turn your wheels."

They showed their mighty strength. "Take it," they said, "convert it, store it. Our strength will give you light and power."

The call of the rivers is persistent. It rings in the ears of Man—and he listens and obeys.

2 Out of the Clouds

If you had asked any of the peoples of old where their particular river came from, they would have said:

"It is heaven-sent. Our river has always been; it will always be. It was made in the beginning."

Not so very long ago we, too, believed that rivers had always been just as we see them today. But now we know better. We know that nothing on the face of the earth lasts forever. Rivers come and go. They have their youth, maturity and old age.

A river's life is much longer than man's; so no one has ever seen a river go through all its stages. But we will telescope time and watch the story from the beginning. And we will start by looking up into the sky. For it is out of the clouds that our river will come.

It starts with rain falling on the land. . . .

We see the rain washing down the nearest slope in thin sheets, then forming into little rills. There are many rills tumbling down every slope. But here where two slopes meet we see their rills join. Now there aren't so many as before, but each is more powerful. Each digs away harder at the land. Each excavates a gully—and the gullies get bigger and bigger. The one we have our eye on is the biggest of all.

As rain rushes down, the rills get bigger and bigger.

When the rains stop, our big gully dries up. But when they come again, a new rill appears in the gully and starts excavating. Year after year the gully gets deeper. At last it is so big that we can't call it a gully any more —it has become a valley.

At first we notice that water runs through our valley only while it is raining and for a little while after. But as the valley gets deeper, we find that the stream stays longer. The reason is that water is seeping in from the sides of the valley. This is rain that sank into the earth. The earth held it like a sponge. Now the sponge is so full that it is letting the water out.

The rains come again and again. Each time the stream stays a little longer and excavates the valley a little deeper. Then at last we see that there is water running through it *all* the time.

"Something more must be feeding the stream," we say.

Something more is. It is water seeping out of the earth again, but now it is coming from a lower level of the earth where much more water is always present in the pores and crevices of the rocks and soil. That is why our stream no longer just pays a visit and goes. With water constantly running in, it has become really established. It is a *permanent* stream.

And we can see that it is going to be a main stream. For while our river was forming, other, smaller streams were forming in neighboring gullies. We see these streams joining up with our stream. From right and left, brooks and rivulets come running in. Like chieftains who bring gifts to their king, these lesser streams come bearing tribute to the main stream.

We call these lesser streams *tributaries*. The tributaries look like the veins of a monstrous leaf joining the midrib. They look like the branches of a mighty tree of which the main stream is the trunk. The monstrous leaf with its veins, the mighty tree with its branches, we call a *river system*. The land which it drains we call a *river basin*.

Our main stream is still in its lusty youth. It is very lively because it is flowing down a steep grade. As it rushes along, it picks up and carries silt and pebbles and even boulders. All of them scour the river channel and deepen it.

As yet the floor of our valley is scarcely any wider than the stream running through it. The valley is shaped like a V, and the river channel is the very bottom of the V. But changes are coming. To a person living be-

Bit by bit, the land slips into the winding river.

side the river, these changes come so slowly that there seems to be no change at all. But in the long history of the earth, it takes only a short time for the valley to widen. For many forces help the river to destroy the land through which it flows. The atmosphere eats away at it. The wind blasts away at it. The rain washes it. The frost cracks it. Particle by particle, the land wastes away—it slips into the river and is carried off to the sea. The valley walls seem to shrink from the river, growing farther and farther apart.

Pretty soon we see that the river no longer fills the whole bottom of the valley. The valley has flattened out like this ⌣. And the river in the valley is swinging

The valley walls seem to grow farther and farther apart.

first to one side then the other. The river looks like a serpent that is wriggling, but not wriggling very hard. The outside of each serpent curve cuts away at the side of the valley because that is where the strong current is—on the outside of each curve.

Watch those loops. For from now on the story of our river will be that the serpent wriggles harder and harder while the valley gets wider and wider. When the loops become deep S curves—which we call *meanders*— and the floor of the valley is wider than any loop, we say that the river is *mature*. When the loops bend over still more so that they look like horseshoes and a whole chain of them swings across the wide valley, we say the river is getting old. An old river does very little cutting. It just plods sleepily along, carrying a great load of silt to the sea. Only in times of flood does it get lively, and then it may wash away the banks or even cut new sections of channel for itself.

But will nothing more happen?

Nobody can say what the future holds for our river. It may be that it will go through many more adventures. The outer zone of the earth, which we call its crust, is never still—it is always rising in one place and sinking in another. If the land through which our river is meandering is lifted up, the stream will grow young again, or be *rejuvenated*, as scientists say. It will start cutting its channel downward again. It will make another V-shaped valley inside the old valley and flatten the new one out as before. The whole story will be repeated.

And suppose the land sinks?

If that happens, then our river is in for trouble. Sea will flow into the valley, and the river will be drowned. Lots of rivers and their valleys have been drowned in the past. San Francisco Bay is a drowned river valley. Chesapeake Bay and the Carolina sounds are drowned river valleys. Most of the bays along the New England coast were cut by streams that afterwards drowned. The

Hudson River is drowned as far up as Troy, New York.

But supposing the land neither rises nor sinks? What will happen then?

In such a case our river is also doomed. Slowly, slowly the land will wear down to a plain. Then the slightest rise in sea level will prove fatal to the valley—it will surely be drowned. In the end the ocean must roll over all.

Eventually the sea will flow into the valley and roll over all.

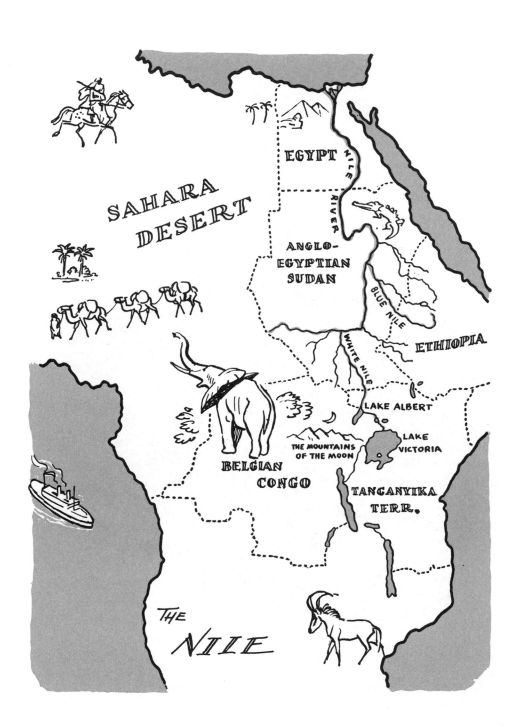

SAHARA DESERT

EGYPT

NILE RIVER

ANGLO-EGYPTIAN SUDAN

BLUE NILE

ETHIOPIA

WHITE NILE

LAKE ALBERT

THE MOUNTAINS OF THE MOON

LAKE VICTORIA

BELGIAN CONGO

TANGANYIKA TERR.

THE NILE

3 Disaster in North Africa

The Nile is the most famous river of the world. It is an African river serving many different peoples. But most particularly it is Egypt's river. For in almost rainless Egypt, only the river makes life possible.

Take the Nile away and Egypt wouldn't exist. It would be just another piece of the Sahara Desert. Take the river away and the wheat, the barley, the millet, the cotton, the date palms and the gardens that delight the eye would disappear. The cities with their trade and industries and arts would vanish, the buildings would crumble slowly into dust. Only a few wandering Bedouins, driving their flocks to some spring-fed oasis, would pass over the burning sand.

How is the river responsible for so much?

It is the Nile that has given Egypt its farm land. And it is the Nile that fertilizes it year after year.

This happens in a most mysterious fashion. About the middle of the summer the river overflows and takes possession of the flat strip of country on either side. For about a hundred days the water stays there. And when at last it goes away, it leaves behind it a very thin, evenly spread layer of rich, black, life-giving mud in which the Egyptian farmer sows his seed. This narrow strip along the river—it is only ten miles wide on the average —together with the fan of land which the river has built about its mouth, is all the farm land Egypt has. Yet this soil is so fertile that it has fed the Egyptians far longer than man has recorded time. Six thousand years ago, when Europe was still a savage hunters' land, fields of grain waved high above the Nile.

The Nile is particularly Egypt's. But it is also everybody's river; for on the banks of the Nile much of mankind's history began. It was here that some of the first

The ancient Egyptians were expert mathematicians.

cities sprang up. Here writing and mathematics and astronomy developed. Here some of the earliest governments were set up. Here was cut the pattern on which we live.

Let us turn back the clock and see the makers of all this when first they came to the river. For they were immigrants. Let us see how and why they and the Nile did such great things together.

It is the end of the last Ice Age, and northern Europe is covered by ice hundreds of feet thick. North Africa is a very different land from the one we know by that name. There is no Sahara Desert. Everything is green,

At the end of the Ice Age, North Africa was rich grassland.

green. It is all parkland and grassland. There is bountiful rain. While mammoth and woolly rhinoceros and reindeer are browsing in southern England and France, North Africa is like a Garden of Eden. Vast herds of antelope and elephant feed here. It is a big-game country. It is a hunters' paradise.

But now the Ice Age passes, and a frightening change begins to come over North Africa. For the rains have shifted northward. The parkland and the grassland begin to dry up. Month after month the pitiless sun beats down and no rain falls. The hungry herds move south. Paradise is fast turning to a desert.

A terrible challenge faces the hunting peoples of

At that time vast herds of elephants and antelopes fed here.

North Africa—they must meet that challenge or die. Some do die. They are paralyzed by the disaster and cannot act—they can neither change their way of life nor go away. Others are made of tougher fiber. They bestir themselves. Some go north, some go south. Some stay where they are, but give up hunting and become wandering shepherds in the land of their fathers.

And some there are who stumble on yet another answer to the drought. Their answer is the boldest of all. It is to take up a new way of life in a new land.

We will keep our eye on these courageous people. For it is they who will create the first cities by the waters of the Nile.

4 A People and Their River

How hopefully they look to the east, these North Africans, pushed out of their home by hunger! In the east, they know lies a region where all is green. Their far-wandering hunters have brought word of it and also of the hippopotamus that can be hunted there.

Yet when they have traveled to the new land, the people's spirits sink. There is a vast carpet of growing things here, indeed, but this is not wholesome parkland and grassland. It is a desolate marsh over which clouds of mosquitoes hang. Was this what their hunters called a river?

Many a man and woman is dismayed by the sight. For there is no clean-channeled river here. The Nile is a formless jungle-swamp, a wide-spreading marsh in which the stream seems to be lost. It is a wilderness of reeds and grasses fifteen and more feet high where horrible crocodiles lie about with open mouths.

But there can be no turning back for these immigrants. There is nothing to return to. Every year in their own land there is less food and less. They must stay here where there is at least the hippopotamus. They will plant seeds. They will nourish the seeds with water from the marsh.

In their homeland these people were wanderers. They didn't plant. They merely gathered fruits and seeds that grew wild. But now, awkwardly and uncertainly, they plant grain. At first they plant only here and there along the edges of the marsh, scooping up the marsh water as best they can to water their little fields. To their joy the grain grows. It grows wonderfully well; for every seed they plant they reap two hundred seeds. Soon the farmers become more ambitious. They get the idea of winning land away from the marshes.

They want to sow bigger and bigger areas with grain. They clear pieces of the jungle-swamp. They dig ditches to drain the water away.

Foot by foot over hundreds, perhaps over thousands, of years the marshes are converted to dry land. The river retreats. It gathers itself together out of the lagoons. It flows faster; it digs a deeper, narrower channel. It learns to run as a river should.

Now there is no question of hunger. In their old hunting life it was always either a feast or a famine for the North Africans. But now there is food that can be stored away for future use. From year to year there is more. In time there is so much that it is no longer necessary for all the people to be farmers. Some can be spared for other tasks, especially now that the Egyptians have invented the plow and put oxen to work. One man makes pots, another weaves cloth, some tan leather, some make bricks. The artisans find it easier to live close together. And so settled communities spring up.

The river is the big problem. Every time it overflows, canals get silted up and have to be dug out again. And more marsh must be continually drained to make new land. These are tasks that call for many hands working together. There must be a plan. There must be leaders to organize the diggers.

And so government is born.

Down at the mouth of the Nile where the river breaks up into many small streams, down where it drops its load of silt, the task is less hard. Here the middle part of the land is a great island between two river branches. The island is shaped like a triangle. It looks like a delta, the fourth letter of the Greek alpha-

At the mouth of the Nile, a triangle of land lies between the two great river branches.

bet. That alphabet has not been invented yet—it will not be born for thousands of years. But some day this formation at the Nile's mouth will be called the Delta. And after it, all similar formations at the mouths of rivers the world over will be called by the same name, whatever their shape.

The Egyptians who live in the Delta call their country Lower Egypt because it is lower down on the river. The people who settle higher up on the river call their country Upper Egypt. Because the river is easier to control in the Delta, Lower Egypt develops more quickly and conquers Upper Egypt. When one king rules over both lands, he has millions of people to gather taxes from. The taxes are in the form of grain. The more grain, the more taxes. Naturally the king is much interested in increasing the amount of grain. He causes all the little local systems of canals to be united in a great national system so that more land can be sown and watered. The Department of Irrigation becomes the very heart of the government.

The river is always in every man's sight. It affects every step of the people's upward climb. To know when they may expect the Nile to overflow, the

Grass from the river swamps was used to make a kind of paper.

Egyptians watch for signs in the sky. They observe the stars and group them into constellations. They learn just how the heavens must look before the flood comes. They work out a calendar.

Now that they know how to measure time, they can keep records of events. They do it by means of pictures. Each picture represents an idea. But in time the pictures come to stand for sounds—and then real writing has been invented.

On what shall the writing be done? Stone, pottery, bone, wood—all are clumsy. The Egyptians look to their river for help, and it does not fail them. There is a tall grass growing in the Nile swamps. It is the papyrus. It grows in thick clumps and rises to a height of 18 feet. Already the Egyptians use it for many things. Now they cut the papyrus stalks into fine strips. They lay the strips crosswise, then beat and press them together into a thin sheet—and they have made paper.

But what will they write with?

The river gives them sharp reeds to use as pens. They take water from the stream and thicken it with vegetable gum. They mix it with soot from fire-blackened pots. And they have ink.

The river spurs the Egyptians on in many directions. It forces them to learn how to measure. For after the flood, dikes may be washed away, ditches may be clogged up, and how can a farmer know where his land ends and his neighbor's begins? At first they measure roughly to settle humble disputes over land. But when they start building, their measurement becomes a science. They learn to measure so exactly that they astonish the world. They put to shame the architects of our own day.

The Egyptians are not building with stone yet. They have no metal tools with which to cut it. They build with sun-dried brick. But time is marching on. Soon they will have copper. With 9-foot jeweled copper saws they will cut the largest blocks of stone ever used for building. They will cut stone so exactly that their architecture will look like jewelers' work except that it will be on a scale of acres not inches. Their tombs and temples will be the wonder of the ages. Long after the ancient Egyptians have passed away, the ruins of their temples and their tombs will stand upon the river bank and awe the world.

The ruins of ancient Egyptian temples stand along the Nile.

5 White Nile and Blue

Less than a hundred years ago the source of the Nile was the biggest puzzle in geography.

"How is it possible for a river to flow through burning desert and not dry up?" people wondered. "In all the land of Egypt no tributaries come to the river's aid, almost no rain falls into it. Yet it arrives at the sea a mighty stream. And once a year it even overflows. What feeds the Nile?"

For two thousand years people had been asking the

same question. But nobody had ever been able to get far enough up the river to find out. There were two arms to the Nile—everybody knew that. One arm was the White Nile. That was the main stream, shrouded in mystery. The other arm was the Blue Nile. That came from Abyssinia—or Ethiopia as it is called now. The explorer James Bruce had traced the Blue Nile to its source in the mountains. He said it was the Blue Nile that brought the rich silt which meant life to the Egyptians. He explained that the silt was so fertile because it was dust washed out of volcanic rocks through which the river cut its way.

But what of the White Nile? Where did it come from? Did it, too, start with little streams up in high mountains?

Back in the days when the Romans ruled Egypt, the Emperor Nero had tried to find out. He had sent out an expedition under two army officers with orders to push up the Nile to its source.

The Roman officers hadn't got to the end of the river, but they had gone farther than anyone else. They came back saying that they had run into marshes. The marshes were so immense and so full of interlaced plants that it was all they could do to get through.

Beyond the marshes they had come to two great rocks over which a river was falling.

But what lay behind the falls? Nobody knew. Did the falls really exist? Nobody knew.

There was one other clue that explorers had to work on. About the same time that the Romans pushed through the marshes, a Greek merchant, Diogenes by name, told about a trading trip he had made. He said he had traveled into Africa overland from the east coast. He had gone inland for twenty-five days. Then he had come to two great lakes and a range of snow mountains. It was his opinion that the snow from those mountains fed the Nile.

The merchant's story had gone down the centuries. Everybody who wrote about the Nile repeated it. The two lakes and the snowy mountains—which came to be called the Mountains of the Moon—took hold of people's imagination like a legend about gold.

But were the lakes and the Mountains of the Moon actually there? The middle of the nineteenth century had already passed, and still nobody had the answer.

Then in the year 1856 John Hanning Speke, an English army officer, started for Africa. He wanted to

A river tumbled over the rocky ledge of the vast range.

make a collection of animals, but at the same time he was curious about the source of the Nile.

"The Mountains of the Moon are probably a vast range stretching right across Africa from east to west," he said to himself. "There I will find the Nile rising in snow as the Ganges rises in the Himalayas."

Speke found something vastly different. On the 28th of January, 1862, he stood looking up at two great

31

Thousands of passenger fish were leaping at the falls.

cliffs between which a river was falling over a rocky ledge.

Blue, shining, 300 yards wide, the stream fell 16½ feet, turned into mad white foam, and sped on. Speke knew he was looking at the Nile. He was watching it as it broke through the lip of Lake Victoria and left it to go on its distant journey to the Mediterranean.

He had not tried to go up the Nile through the marshes. He had struggled inland from the east coast in the same way the Greek Diogenes said he had done. On a previous journey Speke had discovered Lake Victoria and given it its name. He had had a hunch then that somewhere from this huge lake—which is as big as Ireland—he would find the Nile coming out.

On all the rocks native fishermen stood with rod and hook.

And here he was on the spot—thirty miles above the equator.

Lost in thought he stood for hours looking up at the roaring water. He watched the thousands of passenger fish leaping at the falls. He watched the native fishermen standing with rod and hook on all the rocks. In a quiet inlet near the top of the falls he could see hippopotamuses opening their huge pink mouths in lazy yawns. Crocodiles basked in the sun. Cattle were being driven down to drink at the margin of the lake.

"As pretty a scene as one could wish to see," he said to himself.

But it was less of beauty that John Speke was thinking than of what an immense surprise it would be to the world to learn that this was how the Nile began.

Thundering falls pouring out of a monster lake! The whole civilized world thrilled to the discovery. And then more news came. Other explorers had followed Speke, and they had an exciting story to tell. There *were* two lakes, they said. The snows of the Mountains of the Moon *did* feed the Nile. Soon after leaving Lake Victoria, the river flowed into and out of yet another huge body of water—Lake Albert. And this lake was fed not only by rain but also by the melting snows of the Ruwenzori range, which was no other than the Mountains of the Moon. The story Diogenes had told was true in every respect!

With such great reservoirs behind it, the Nile is safe. It can flow thousands of miles under the burning sun and yet arrive at the sea a mighty river.

But here is the curious thing. It is not the White Nile, fed by the two lakes, that causes the yearly flood. The business of the lakes is merely to keep the river full—they have nothing to do with the overflow. That is the work of the Blue Nile—of the Blue Nile and the Atbara, a smaller tributary also coming from Abyssinia.

Without these two the Nile would never overflow in spite of all its vast reserves.

If you were to see the Blue Nile and the Atbara in the dry months of the year, you wouldn't believe they have anything to do with the flood. In the ten dry months of each year, the Blue Nile becomes so shallow that it is quite unnavigable. The Atbara dries up altogether. Then the rains begin up in Abyssinia, and for two months the rivers become raging torrents. The change comes so suddenly that it seems like a miracle every time it happens.

Captain Samuel Baker, who discovered Lake Albert and explored the Atbara River, tells how his men were once almost trapped by the suddenness with which the water came.

For days his party had been moving along the river bed. It was perfectly dry and sunbaked except for a pool here and there. Water had remained only in the very deep holes that had been dug out in the channel by the river itself when it rushed through in its force.

One night—it was the 24th of June—when many of his men were sleeping on the clean sand of the river bed, the explorer and his wife suddenly heard a rumbling sound like distant thunder. The roar increased until it woke the men. Some of them rushed into camp shouting, "The river, the river!" Everybody was up in a moment. And in the intense confusion the interpreter explained that the noise they heard was not thunder— it was the river coming down! The last of the men were still scrambling up the steep bank. They were only just in time to reach the top before a wall of water was upon them in the darkness.

When morning broke, Captain Baker stood upon the banks of a noble river, the wonder of the desert. Yesterday there had been a sheet of glaring sand with a fringe of withered bushes and trees on its borders. In one night a mysterious change had taken place. The wasted river had become a magnificent stream some 500 yards wide and 15 to 20 feet deep.

Down in Egypt the engineers would soon be measuring the height of the river Nile and sending the word along. Farmers would watch the river change color as the dust from the volcanic rocks poured in. Soon now the overflow would be taking place—the rains were falling and the snows were melting in Abyssinia.

6 Highlights

You may think of the Nile as beginning at Ripon Falls if you like. But geographers start farther back. They say the Kagera River, which flows into Lake Victoria from the west, is a piece of the Nile. If you object that the Kagera flows into the lake 200 miles from the falls, they will answer:

"It makes no difference. That's the way we regard other rivers with a lake between them. We think of the rivers as flowing *through* a lake. In this case the

Giraffes, water buffalo and antelope crowd to the river's edge.

distance is longer, that's all."

Either way, the Nile is still the most exciting river in the world. It has so much to show that it is impossible to take in everything. But the highlights stand out.

Watch the river making its greatest leap in the Murchison Falls just before reaching Lake Albert. The Nile comes raging furiously through a rockbound pass. Suddenly it drops. The cleft it squeezes through is only 19 feet wide. The plunge in three cascades is 400 feet.

Even elephants and hippopotamuses play in the water.

The Murchison Falls take our breath—there is something about great falls that makes the heart beat fast.

Immediately beyond is a different kind of wonder. Crocodiles by the thousand lie sunning on the bank. Hippopotamuses amuse themselves in the water. The rhinoceros, the buffalo, lions and leopards, elephants in dozens, antelope in herds of all sizes, wart hogs, monkeys—all come to the Nile to drink. This region is their preserve.

Lake Albert is salty. But the Nile makes so short a

journey through it that the river comes out of the lake almost sweet. Five miles through the lake, and again the river is on its way. For a while it flows calmly along, but soon mountains close in upon it. Again it becomes a torrent that rages and roars and rushes madly downhill over the rapids. Then another change—the Nile has entered the plain. Just a little more and we are at the strangest part of the river.

We have reached the Sudd, the region of the terrible marshes through which the Roman soldiers struggled. We look around and cannot believe our eyes—the river has melted away, it has disappeared. As far as we can see in every direction there is swamp covered with a thick growth of water weeds. The Nile has lost itself in a maze of channels. The river, which farther back was often walled in by cliffs rising 180 feet, now has no banks at all. It has spread to a width of fifteen miles. Hither and thither shift the floating islands of vegetation as the winds uproot them. The lagoons open and close. The river is navigable, yes, but only for the rare master pilot who knows where to find it. We wonder that anyone can.

Here 25,000 square miles are under water most of the year, and it seems beyond the power of man to change this state of things. Attempts are made. Engineers come in steamers and ram stakes into the floating islands. Then they tie ropes to the stakes, put their engines in reverse, and pull the lumps of growth away. Once the English cleared five miles of the Sudd. They worked with five steamers and eight hundred men. It took them three months to clear the five miles.

And yet think of it! The ancient Egyptians conquered a great jungle-swamp just like this. For the Sudd, scholars tell us, is a good picture of what the lower Nile must have been like when the North African hunters came to it long ago. They didn't clear five miles in three months—of that we can be certain. They had no steamers. They had no metal spades even. With their bare hands and the rudest of tools, they cleared the floating vegetation away.

But let us go on and see what lies beyond the Sudd.

A bird paradise is ahead of us. It is the second on the way. There was one on a bushy island at the very top of Ripon Falls, and there will be yet another in the Delta. But it is to this middle ground, halfway along the river's course, that many of the migrant birds from Europe come to spend the winter. Countless millions of them are here. They soar and swoop, flutter

On the Upper Nile thousands of cranes wade on the shore.

and call. They don't mate or build nests though they see the native African birds raising families. The migrants have come only for food and rest. They keep to themselves. The native birds do, too. They neither fly nor play nor fight with the visitors but go on peacefully living their lives.

The Nile is almost in the desert now, and through it the river cuts an enormous S. For there is granite below that bars its way. At the First Cataract—which is really the fifth we have met coming down river— the Nile straightens out. But here something else stops it. It is the great Aswan Dam.

Why did men throw this wall across the Nile when water is needed so badly in Egypt?

You may be sure it is to make farming still better. The dam makes possible an *even* flow of water through the year. The wall holds back the river for 200 miles and forms a lake that can be drawn on at will. Whenever the farmers need more water for irrigation, sluice gates are opened up and the water comes through. With this even flow, not only can more land be irrigated, but three or four harvests can be reaped on the same ground. In winter the farmers harvest cereals, in summer cotton and rice.

Everywhere along the river bank we see people drawing up the life-giving water. Indeed, we can *hear* them doing it, for the primitive water wheels the farmers use to raise the Nile water up the ten- or twelve-foot bank creak and whine ceaselessly. Each upright wheel has a chain of twenty or more red earthenware pitchers attached to its rope rim. As the wheel turns, the pitchers sink into the Nile, are filled, and reaching the highest point, empty into a trough that leads to a ditch and so to the farmer's field. Up on the bank a man drives a pair of oxen round and round to make the wheel go. Ten hours a day, eight months of the year the weary toil goes on. And there are thousands of such wheels in Egypt.

At Aswan we are already in the land of the ancient Egyptians, and now there are countless of their mighty works on both sides of the Nile.

Once the city of Thebes, capital of ancient Egypt, stood not far below Aswan. The sacred Nile ran right through the royal city. On one bank lived the kings in their luxurious palaces, with the hum of busy life around them. On the other bank stood the temples of the gods. The luxurious palaces have all crumbled to dust, but the stone temples remain. Thousands of people travel over oceans and continents to see them.

Even more travelers, however, come to pay their respects to the Pyramids, those three gigantic royal tombs which, together with the Sphinx, stand farther down the river. The Greeks called the Pyramids the "First of the Seven Wonders of the World." And they still are that. There is no building on earth to match them for exactness. Imagine huge blocks of stone cut so perfectly that the mortar needed to hold them together is thin as a sheet of paper!

Nor is there any building to match them in bulk. The Great Pyramid measures more than half a mile

The Great Pyramid is as tall as a forty-story skyscraper.

around the base. It covers 13½ acres. Six milllion tons of stone were quarried to build it. If those slabs were cut into blocks a foot square and set end to end in a straight line, they would stretch two-thirds of the way around the globe at the equator!

There is a question which every visitor asks:

"How did the ancient Egyptians ever do it without machines?"

We who watched the North African hunters struggle with the Nile don't need to ask. For all it took to build the Pyramids was patience, skill, and organization; and we know where the Egyptians got those. They met the river's challenge. It made them into the mightiest builders the world has seen.

The
AMAZON

7 Much Space, Few People

The Amazon flows right across the top of South America. The river is so powerful that it pushes out over a hundred miles before it mingles with the Atlantic. Out at sea sailors recognize the stream by its yellow color. "The Amazon!" they cry joyfully. They know they are nearing the continent.

It was the gold-hungry Spaniards who first explored this mighty jungle river, stumbling on it just by chance. Rumor said that somewhere east of the

Gold-hungry Spaniards were the first to explore the Amazon.

Andes lay a country of fabulous riches, ruled over by
El Dorado, The Gilded King, whose body sparkled
with golden sequins as the sky with stars. The Spaniards
were looking for this wondrous land where building
stones were riveted with silver and palaces were roofed
with gold. Needless to say, they didn't find it. But, led
by one Francisco Orellana, some fifty of them did have a
never-to-be-forgotten adventure. Fighting, starving,
despairing, hoping, enduring, they went all the way
down the 3,900-mile river.

It might well have been named Orellana's River.

They had heard that beyond the Andes lay a land of riches.

And so it was at first. But after a while people began to call it the river of the Amazons, for as the story of the great adventure was told again and again, one part stood out. It was the part where the Spaniards in a fierce battle saw—or thought they saw—Indian women fighting in the front ranks. It seemed a very astonishing thing to the Spaniards to behold women with bows and arrows in their hands, acting as captains and outdoing the men. The Amazons, as the Spaniards called the fighting women, naturally took hold of people's imagination. In the end they gave the river its name.

All About Great Rivers of the World

Though not the longest, the river of the Amazons is the mightiest stream on earth. It bears to the sea *one-fifth of all the running water in the world*!

Where does the river get so much?

Not from its source, which is a little snow-fed lake in the Andes, less than a hundred miles from the Pacific and half way up to the sky. Much more of the Amazon's water comes from tributary streams. There are 1,100 of them. They bring tribute from Venezuela, Colombia, Ecuador, Peru, Bolivia, Brazil. Seven of the rivers are over 1,000 miles long. The Madeira River is 2,000, and before it joins the main stream has 90 tributaries of its own.

Everything about the Amazon speaks of its might. It is so wide that for most of its course it divides in two, with tens of thousands of islands between the channels. In its lower course it is 40 miles across. Its huge mouth holds three islands, one of them as big as Switzerland.

The river is very deep, too. Ocean steamers can go all the way up to the city of Iquitos in Peru. That is 2,300 miles from the sea. Geographers say the great depth of the river explains the current. The Amazon has so much water that it can speed along for hundreds of miles *almost on a level plane.*

"Such a powerful river must carry a lot of silt. It must have built a huge delta," you think.

True, the Amazon takes out into the Atlantic millions of tons of silt a year. But it has no delta. For while the river is strong, the ocean is strong, too. The river brings down silt and drops it, but the ocean currents keep carrying it away.

Indeed, the sea even invades the river's province. The rise and fall of the tide can be felt 500 miles upstream. At times an unusually high tide sets in toward the shore, and then there is a real battle between river and ocean. The water piles up in a great wave known as a *bore.* The breaking wall of water comes up river 5 to 12 feet high and moving very fast. It sweeps up the Amazon for as much as a hundred miles. Fortunately this destructive wave announces itself as it comes with a roar that can be heard for miles. So people on the river have a chance to get away.

Actually there are very few people on the river. There are extremely few in the whole Amazon basin. Probably in all that vast space there are not more human beings than in the city of Chicago—three million or so. Most of them are in Brazil.

But why is this? You would think the Amazon and its tributaries would be busy avenues of communication. You would think steamers would be plying back and forth all the time, bringing goods into the interior and taking back the products of the region.

There is very little traffic. For one thing, the rivers are not navigable all the way up. There are perilous rapids that stretch for as much as 200 miles, and only skillful natives can get by them in their canoes.

But there are other and more powerful reasons. The Amazon lies near the equator, which means it is hot in the lowlands even in the rainy season. Also it is very humid. Two hundred inches of rain fall in an average year. That is five times the rain that falls in New York City and ten times as much as in San Francisco. In this humid heat the standing puddles and pools breed countless millions of mosquitoes; so the whole area is a hotbed of disease, particularly of malaria and yellow fever, which are carried by mosquitoes.

Added to this is the jungle. The jungle is perhaps the main reason why so few human beings go up and down the 30,000 and more miles of navigable waterways. The jungle is why you see no bridges or dams or dikes or levees on the river, no busy factories, no sawmills, no large-scale fisheries, no agriculture such as we know. The Amazon jungle, which is the biggest forest on earth, is a bar to all these things.

For nowhere else do plants crowd so as here. The air is so warm and humid that things grow as if they were in a huge hothouse. The immense jungle that results gives man no chance. Elsewhere man conquers the forest. Here the forest conquers man. Plant life here is too vigorous to be subdued by his feeble machete, or his ax, or even his electric saw. Man has not even been able to make paths in the jungle because they grow over almost as soon as he makes them. Here the rivers are the only paths from one settlement to another, for there is no *land*. Everything is forest. And the bits man has cleared make no more difference in the whole than a few weeds pulled out of a mile-long corn field.

The Amazon is unfortunately placed. Mightiest of rivers though it is, it plays only a small part in the work of the world. For the Amazon flows through a region where human beings count for little and plants and insects count for much.

8 In the Amazon Jungle

What does the jungle look like? What makes it different from other forests?

If you look at it from a river boat, you can't really see the jungle. All you behold is a wall of green. Above you is the blue sky, below is the yellow water, and along the side the wall of green. The trees are all overhung with ropelike lianas. These are parasite vines that climb and twine and weave everything together. They make you think of a ship's rigging with the trunks of the trees for masts and the branches for yards. Here and there you can pick out a towering giant or a few palms that look like huge green feathers, but that's all you can distinguish beyond the fringe of the forest. What lies behind is all mystery.

You have to go *into* the jungle to see what is there. And when you do, the meaning of this tropical forest slowly comes over you. The jungle is a place in which the most intense kind of struggle is going on for light and life. It is root against root, stem against stem, leaf against leaf. Plants push and crowd and reach above one another. They fill all the space up and up till every level is choked with growth. There is so much of it that everything is one dense, tangled mass, a living web woven together by lianas. You can't walk in a straight line anywhere. In some areas you can't even see what is behind the nearest tangle until you have cut your way through, or gone under, or around.

Life is very busy in the everlasting twilight of this tropical forest. But death is busy here, too. You know that because there is the trunk of a fallen tree to remind you. It has lost out in the struggle for life. And you can guess what may have happened, for you see a tree being killed right before your eyes. It has fallen

In the Amazon jungle you see four distinct levels of plants.

into the grip of a parasite. The parasite has sucking disks that drain the tree's sap. The vines enlace the tree, go from branch to branch.

"Soon," you think, "the tree will die and fall and lie like this log at our feet. And it took perhaps hundreds of years to grow!"

But what need of pity here? What is one tree or a hundred where there are countless millions? This is the Amazon jungle. It stretches from the Atlantic Ocean all the way across South America to the Andes Mountains.

Now that your eyes have become accustomed to the dim, gray-green light, you notice that there are distinct levels of plants in the jungle, four different stories of

The fourth story is made of great trees whose tops face the sky.

leaves. The floor of the forest is covered with a carpet of low-growing things. They are so thick that they hide from view the fallen tree. You would not have known it was there, perhaps, had you not stumbled. Above the carpet rise bushes and slender palms. The third story is of shade-loving trees. Different kinds of palms and the chocolate tree are here, laden with perching ferns and cacti. And above them rises the fourth story, made up of the great trees whose tops face the sky and spread out like a canopy above all the other growth.

You look about you and try to count the different kinds of plants in this forest above a forest. But you soon lose track.

"There must be more different ones here than any-where else in the world!" you think.

And you are right. Nearly nine-tenths of all the growing things in the world are represented in the Amazon basin.

The variety in the jungle is bewildering. Very seldom will you find two trees of the same kind side by side. We who live in the temperate zone are used to seeing large stands of one kind of tree. We know oak forests and pine forests. Or we know forests that have a dozen kinds of trees at most, repeated over and over again. In the Amazon forest, though you will once in a while find a stand of palms or laurel, you will see hundreds of different kinds of trees all jumbled together. In most regions there will be scores of different kinds on a single acre. One scientist counted 117 different woods on a piece of jungle half a mile square.

Some other things stand out, too. There is a very long distance between the ground and the first branches of the trees. To make up for that, a great many trees have their trunks supported by buttresses, the way some old churches are. Or the trees have prop roots that give them a very wide look at the base. There are

very few soft woods. And there are comparatively few evergreens. Yet the jungle is always green in every season of the year; for there is no seasonal falling of leaves. The jungle is so warm all the time that trees have no need to strip and go into hibernation.

A huge, glittering, blue butterfly makes its way toward you. You are astonished at its size and beauty. But it isn't rare here. This is butterfly country. You will see more butterflies along the Amazon than anywhere else in the world. In all of Europe there are only 321 kinds; and here, within an hour's walk of the Brazilian city of Belém, one scientist collected 700 kinds.

Insects share honors with the plants in the jungle. There is every imaginable kind of insect here, from the seven-inch butterfly and the six-inch beetle to the tiny gnat that is no bigger than a speck of dust. This is where you will see processions of sauba ants. These amazing creatures cut leaves with their jaws and carry the bits home to their nests, each ant holding its round bit of leaf up like a parasol. This is where you will see columns of army ants on the march. And when you do, you will let them have the right of way. For army ants on a raid are not to be interfered with. When

This greatly enlarged picture shows how sauba ants carry
round bits of leaves.

they enter a settlement, the natives just pick up their
children and their pets and leave. It is better to run
away from army ants than to fight them.

That butterfly you saw is as beautiful a thing as
you will see in the jungle. The insect is all the more
striking because there is so little color in this tropical
forest. Perhaps you have heard otherwise, but actually
there is very little color except green in the jungle.
To be sure, there are some brilliant and amazing flowers; yet you seldom come upon a great mass of color.
And that is very understandable; for the flowers of
the trees are themselves generally green, and even when
they aren't, they fall very quickly. One day a tree
will be in bloom; next day it has already finished
blooming, and for another twelve months it will bear
no more flowers.

No, the jungle is not colorful. You do not say,
"How beautiful this is!" Instead you think, "How

Howler monkeys scream as a boa constrictor threatens.

gloomy, how immense, how lonely! And how silent!"

For there is almost no sound. You do not hear the cheerful noises of our northern forests—the scurrying of squirrels among dead leaves, the scolding of chipmunks, the beat of hoofs as a deer bounds over dry ground. No reassuring sound of ax or saw intrudes, no whistle of distant train or whir of airplane. Once in a while a bird calls. Or the silence may be broken by the sudden scream of some unwary creature caught by a jaguar or a boa constrictor. Howler monkeys

Beside the river a jaguar pounces on a helpless capybara.

raise a din morning and evening. A tree or some great bough may crash. And there will be occasional noises that you cannot explain. There is one like the clang of an iron bar against a hollow tree.

"It is the Curupira, the spirit of the forest," Indians say when they hear that sound. The Curupira makes all the noises Indians cannot explain.

Immense, gloomy, lonely, and silent. That is the impression the jungle makes—even on scientists for whom it is filled with interest. Is it strange that natives cling to the rivers and seldom go far inland?

There was, indeed, one time when the jungle and its mighty network of rivers woke up in spite of all the difficulties set in the way of man. That was during the great rubber boom when the newly invented bicycle and automobile called for rubber and only the Amazon jungle could supply it. But as soon as the cultivated rubber groves of the East got into production, the boom was over. For jungle rubber cannot compete with cultivated rubber. On a plantation, rubber is easy and cheap to gather because the trees are all together. In the jungle there is perhaps one rubber tree to an acre.

Yet it may be that the great forest will again resound with human voices and busy traffic may once more ply up and down the Amazon. For the jungle holds many valuable things besides rubber. It has a rich variety of woods—from balsa, the lightest of all, to the precious "ax-breaking" woods that are so heavy they sink in water. There are Brazil nuts and cashew nuts. There are a great many vegetable oils. There is arnotto for coloring butter and cheese. There is carnauba wax, which is used in shoe polish, furniture waxes and phonograph records. There are resins and fibers and tree gums and medicinal plants. If science will only get after the insects, the great forest may cease to be jungle and the Amazon may take its rightful place among the trade rivers of the world.

Deep in the jungle men gathered rubber and smoked the great balls over a smouldering fire.

TIBET

C H I N A

CHUNGKING   ICHANG

YANGTZE RIVER

NANKING

HANKOW

SHANGHAI

The

YANGTZE

9 China's Main Street

A heavily laden Chinese junk is moving up the Yangtze-Kiang. The ship is going very slowly, for it has reached the most difficult part of the way. It is in the dangerous Yangtze gorges, where steep cliffs shut the river in on either side and the water foams and boils in rapids and whirlpools.

Look high up on the face of the cliff and you will see a terrible, yet inspiring, sight. A path has been cut along the cliff. The path is so narrow that blows would not drive horse or donkey or ass to go there. Yet along that path a gang of seventy or eighty men are

struggling. They are bent almost double with the strain of what they are doing. Their hands as well as their feet touch the ground. The men are harnessed to a rope. Follow it down, and you will see that it is attached to the ship. The men are towing the junk up river.

It is a terrible thing to see human beings working like galley slaves of old. It is terrible to see them risking their lives where beasts would refuse to go. But there is something grand about it, too. For those men bent double on the towpath are a symbol. They shout

Men harnessed to a rope tow the junk up the Yangtse River.

aloud man's triumph over Nature. In the Yangtze gorges, man has conquered earth's most difficult river.

"But is it worth-while," you ask, "to conquer a river at such cost?"

"We have no choice," the Chinese will answer you. "We cannot live without The River—it is our one great waterway. Dozens of our largest cities and hundreds of smaller towns and villages have only this one outlet to the sea. Half the commerce of all China moves along The River."

The River. That is what millions call it—simply

Kiang. Or they call it *Ta Kiang*, Great River. Or *Chang Kiang*, Long River. Nobody is in any doubt as to which river is meant. For the Yangtze is China's Main Street. It runs right across the country west to east, cutting it into two equal parts. It drains one-third of the land. In the Yangtze basin live 200,000,-000 people—one-tenth of the human race. *The River* is name enough for such a stream.

How shall we regard it, then, among the rivers of the world? The Yangtze is not the longest, it is not the widest, it is not the mightiest river. Where shall we place it?

We must give it the honored first place as the most important river of all, for it serves more people than any other, and serves them vitally. In every sense the Yangtze is China's life stream. It isn't just a trade river, a highway along which goods are picked up and distributed. It is an agricultural river as well. If you look down at the Yangtze from an airplane, you will see that the river is used to irrigate millions of farms through all the center of the land.

A network of ditches stretches out from the river. From above, the ditches look like the streets of a city. The ditches reach out to tiny plots, garden-size farms,

As he walks the tread wheel, he pumps water to the rice fields.

where men and women toil endlessly with ages-old hand tools—planting, transplanting, fertilizing, weeding, harvesting, raising the family's food, raising food for the nation. Everywhere south of the Yangtze you will see farmers working the tread wheel to pump water into long wooden troughs to flood their paddy fields; for south of the Yangtze lies China's rice bowl. To the north it is wheat and millet and beans.

Strangely, this river on which one-tenth of mankind depends runs almost half its course before it has any meaning for human beings at all. Its beginning is somewhere high up in the wild country north of Tibet. The stream hurtles down from a three-mile height, then goes surging and tumbling for hundreds of miles through a deep, gloomy trench. The Yangtze fills its trench from side to side. It foams and roars between the high steep walls that imprison it. It rages through terrifying shadows. It is untamed and untamable.

Suddenly the river turns north, then zigzags eastward. It picks up tributaries. It meets mountains and cuts deep gorges through them. Only in the last 1,000 miles of its 3,200-mile journey, does it become the sunny and cheerful river that is China's blessing.

Once out of the gorges, an abrupt change takes place. The river winds and winds through rich soil that once lay under the sea. Gone is loneliness. Now cities, towns, villages and farms line the banks. There are still treacherous sandbanks for ships to worry about, but from now on the river is full of traffic. Clumsy junks, sampans with patched sails, fishing craft, rafts, steamers of all sizes ply up the river and down. Houseboats are moored together by the thousand, forming vast floating cities. The river they ride on is a deep yellow, for it has picked up silt which colors it. At its mouth the Yangtze will drop its yellow load

Thousands of Chinese live on houseboats moored on the river.

to build out a great delta. Far out the silt will color the East China Sea.

Scholars tell us it was not on this busy main highway that Chinese civilization began but on another long river to the north. This is the Hwang Ho, the river we call Yellow and the Chinese speak of as their Sorrow because its floods come so often and are so terrible. There is no great traffic on the Hwang Ho, for it is all choked up with sand bars. But clearly this wasn't always so. Some 2,500 years ago the ancient Chinese took the trouble to build a canal to link the Hwang Ho with the Yangtze. Later on they even extended the Grand Canal north to Peiping and south to Hangchow, making the whole canal 1,200 miles long. Part of the Grand Canal is now silted up. But the part between the rivers is still used. It is an everlasting reminder of what marvelous engineers the Chinese were long ago.

Scholars say that civilization started on the Hwang Ho just the way the Egyptian civilization did—out of the need to work together to control the river. For even then China's Sorrow was carrying down avalanches of yellow mud each summer. The mud would choke up the channel and cause the river to overflow. It would drown villages and farms. The Chinese engineers racked their brains. What could they do about it? Then an engineer named Yu had an idea. Instead of building up the banks, he decided to dredge the channel. He succeeded so well that he was made Emperor of China.

It is said that Yu worked nine years to lead the waters of the river back to their proper channel. In those nine years he thought neither of food nor of drink nor of what to put on. He was so taken up with his work that he would pass by the door of his own house and not look in even when he could hear his little son crying inside. The Chinese remember Yu to this day in an old saying: "How grand was the achievement of Yu! How far-reaching his glorious energy! But for Yu, we should all have been fishes."

Today the river which Yu kept under control is one of the great killers of mankind. For famine follows the floods and kills more than the river drowns. The problem of silt is harder to handle all the time. The river bed builds up and up. In some stretches so much silt collects that *every year* the dikes have to be raised five or six feet.

The Yangtze, too, has to be diked. All through its lower course the river flows through man-made walls. And though it is far less destructive than the Hwang Ho, the Yangtze isn't always well-behaved. Every once in a while it, too, goes on a rampage and breaks through at some point. Then villages are destroyed, cities are damaged, thousands of square miles of farm land are covered with water. In the flood of 1931 at least 150,000 people lost their lives.

But the Chinese are a patient people. They don't complain about the Yangtze. In comparison with the Hwang Ho, it seems a merciful river to them. They take its floods almost as a matter of course. Those who understand such things talk about a dam that could be built to hold the waters back in the gorges. But the farmers know nothing of that.

"The River Dragons are angry," they say when the river breaks through the defenses. They just pick up their children and anything else they can carry and go camp on the dikes. When the river goes down, they return. They rebuild their mud houses, plant again, fill in the gaps in the dikes, and go on living as before. They take the bad with the good. Even an occasional flood seems a small price to pay for all The River does for them.

"The River Dragons are angry," they shout as the flood breaks.

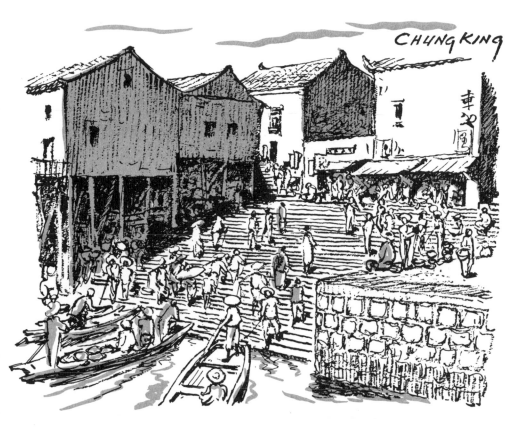

10 Junk in the Yangtze Gorges

During the Second World War, when the Japanese overran China, the Chinese government moved to Chungking.

"The enemy can never take it," the Chinese thought. "They won't be able to get up The River through the gorges."

The Japanese took Shanghai near the river's mouth. They moved up and took the capital, Nanking. They took Hankow, the Pittsburgh of China. They took every town on the Yangtze right up to Ichang, the gateway to the gorges. But they couldn't get beyond.

For probably there isn't a more dangerous river voyage anywhere on earth than the 350-mile stretch between the cities of Ichang and Chungking. On that short trip there isn't a junk that hasn't had at least one hair-breadth escape. One out of ten is badly damaged. One out of twenty is wrecked. How many lives are lost is unknown.

And yet, if you will believe it, there are people who take the trip from Ichang to Chungking just for the fun of it. For there is no more exciting scenery on earth than the Yangtze gorges. Imagine mile after mile of cliffs thousands of feet high shutting in the wild, rock-strewn river. Some cliffs are purple, some are gray, some bright green with trees and scrub, some with tiny terraced farms that look like pieces of jig-saw puzzle. And through the swirling water, imagine a junk struggling against the current, fighting every inch of the way. It looks tiny against the background of the towering cliffs.

What does it take in human effort, in skill and sweat and anxiety, to carry sixty tons of cargo through this awe-inspiring scenery?

Under the best conditions, that struggling little ship will make the trip from Ichang to Chungking in 25 days, traveling between dawn and sunset—for nothing can move on the upper Yangtze at night. That will be 14 miles a day. If the river is low and the wind contrary, the journey may take as long as 60 days— 6½ miles between dawn and sunset. We could *walk* 6½ miles in two hours!

The junk isn't pretty to look at. It is a freight ship, and nothing is expected of it except that it get there. Low, square-nosed, with a high stern, it is about 120 feet long by a dozen wide. Besides cargo, it carries the skipper and his family, whose home this is, and around a hundred men. Some seventy or eighty of the crew are trackers, the fellows who do the towing. And there they are on the perilous path cut in the face of the cliff.

The men are nearly naked. Their bodies are bent, every muscle taut. Each tracker has a short piece of bamboo rope around his body, and this rope is fastened by a slip knot to the bamboo towrope. The rope is very strong, but it may break. Then a tracker has to be quick to slip the knot if he is to save himself from being dragged down. The men are in single file, one on one side of the rope, the next man on the other. They are chanting a singsong phrase to keep in step.

Running up and down the line with pieces of split bamboo in their hands are three gangers. They are the foremen of the gang. They see to it that the trackers keep moving once they have started. Otherwise the ship may slip into the strong current and drag them all into the water, perhaps to their death. The gangers shout and bring the bamboo stick down on the back of the slackers—you can tell who is pulling and who isn't. But all the time the foremen are straining to hear the sound of a drum that comes up to them from the junk. The drum sends up instructions—when to move, when to halt. For there are times when the trackers must stop.

Away in the rear three men are spread out at a distance from one another. Their eyes are on the 1,200-foot towrope, which is constantly catching on boulders and pieces of rock that stick out. These men's business is to keep the line clear. Many a one of them has had a bad fall. Many a one has had broken bones. It is dangerous work climbing along ragged rocks to

His business is to throw the towline clear of the rocks.

push off the rope before it gets chafed to pieces by the heavy boat tugging at its lower end.

But much more dangerous is the work of the naked men you see perched on the rocks 'way out in the swift-running river. Their business is to wade or swim behind the towline and throw it clear of the rocks. Every hour of the day these strong swimmers risk their lives. Many a time in these gorges they have swum out with a cord around their bodies to rescue a drifting junk whose towrope has broken. They perform feats of valor all day long. They have the deep respect of the crew. . . . But what of the junk?

There she is, inching along. She is trying to round the point of a great reef that goes halfway across the river. On one side of the junk the water is pouring like a millrace. On the other side are swirling eddies. The pilot, standing on the foredeck, is rapping out orders to the fifteen or sixteen men beside him who are frantically working the great bowsweep to help guide the craft.

At the foot of the mast the drummer squats on his haunches with the drum between his knees. He is beating a tattoo with a couple of sticks. It is the trackers' signal that all's well. Should the towline get caught, or should anything else go amiss, he will instantly change the rhythm.

On a raised platform in the tiller room stands the helmsman, his hands grasping the 14-foot tiller. He is a practical expert, this pilot. He knows nothing of instruments; he never looks at a compass. He just knows the Yangtze. He has been up and down this river so many times that he knows every rock and whirlpool in it. It is uncanny the way he can "read" the water—tell from the look of the surface what lies underneath it.

He doesn't fight the river—he coaxes it. Down be-

The helmsman uses a 14-foot tiller to pilot this Chinese junk.

low, between Hankow and Ichang, where the sand banks lie, he didn't try to breast the current. He took the junk continually backward and forward across the channel, knowing well that it would take twice as long to reach Chungking if he "bucked" the river. And here in the gorges he makes use of every current, every swirl, every backwash. He watches for signs and takes advantage of them, too. On the face of the cliff he sees white figures on a tarred background—they help him to judge how high the water is. In the gorges the water may rise 50 feet in a single day. At high level it may be 100 feet above low.

And where is the skipper?

He is perched on top of the deckhouse, anxiously watching everything that's going on. At the moment, his eyes are glued to the reef. His heart is in his mouth as the junk starts to round the point. The water is low, and the rocks jut out of it like so many dragons. Will the pilot make allowance enough? Will the towrope hold? If it breaks now, destruction is certain; for there, just astern, is another reef waiting to smash his drifting vessel.

Above the torrent's roar he hears the pilot on the foredeck giving commands. The sailors beside him pull desperately on the bowsweep. The drum beats. Up on the cliff the trackers are gripping the ground with their hands as they strain every muscle to make progress. The gangers run excitedly up and down. The junk keeps forging ahead. One foot. Another foot. Slowly it creeps by the dragons.

Relief spreads over the skipper's face, but next instant the anxious look is back again. There is so much to worry about! Rocks and reefs and eddies. Water level always changing. Current up to 13 miles an hour. Towrope forever catching. Towrope always in danger of breaking—in spite of all the care it gets, in spite of his laying out money for a new one every trip. Whirl-

The junk got caught in a whirlpool and was swept right around.

pools. Get caught in one of those and it's all over with you—you can never pull out. There was that junk two days ago. Got caught in a whirlpool and swept right around, by bad luck just as a steamer was coming on. The junk struck it athwart the bow. If it hadn't been for the lifeboats stationed at that dangerous spot, many more would have drowned.

And rapids. Twenty major rapids between Ichang and Chungking, no two alike, each having to be tackled in a different way. The skipper knows he has the best pilot on the river—but still. . . . That last rapid just before Chungking, that New Dragon Rapid which, they say, formed in his father's time when part of the foothills broke away and slid into the river— that's the worst of them. From 800 yards the channel suddenly narrows to 200, and the squeezed-in river comes raging through like a water chute. There's something to make a brave man's heart leap to his throat. Three men are lost at that rapid every day in the year, they say.

The junk is approaching a bend in the river where a signal station is located. The station is signaling: "Steamer coming down!"

The steamer has the right of way. Already the pilot is guiding the junk to the side. More delay. Then there will be the wash to contend with. Sometimes after a steamer has passed through a rapid, the wash is so bad it's an hour before the junk gets under way.

A nasty lot, those steamers. But the skipper envies them, too. They have so much easier a time of it in the gorges than the junks do. To be sure, even the most powerful can't get through the worst rapids without trackers sometimes. But a steamer can do the 350 miles in three days. Three days! Think of it!

The future, he knows, belongs to the steamboats; but the future is far away, the skipper thinks. He will go up and down many times before the future sweeps the junks from the upper river. He is stirred by those awesome gorges which call for everything vessel and man can do. He is proud of his ugly, hard-working, all-enduring ship—he wouldn't trade it for a steamer. No! He was born on a junk. He will die on a junk.

A steamer has a much easier time of it through the gorges.

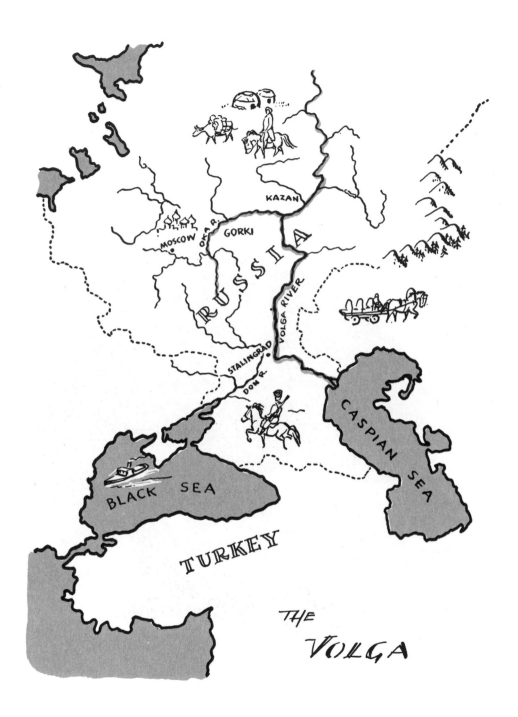

MOSCOW

OKA R.

GORKI

KAZAN

RUSSIA

VOLGA RIVER

STALINGRAD

DON R.

BLACK SEA

CASPIAN SEA

TURKEY

THE
VOLGA

11 Out Into the World

If you look at the map of Europe, you will see that compared with England, France, Spain, Italy, and Greece, Russia has very little coastline. And even such coastline as she does have isn't much use to her. On the north are the Arctic Ocean and the White Sea. They are frozen nine months of the year. The Gulf of Finland is frozen half the time. Even the Caspian Sea is often frozen in its northern part. And the Sea of Azov is little better than a marsh.

All About Great Rivers of the World

If not for her rivers, what would Russia have been? It is her rivers that have kept her from being a bottled-up country. It is her rivers that have taken her out into the world. And of all of them the Volga has served her best. It is the longest, it is the widest. It isn't hampered by rapids the way the Dnieper River is. Unbroken and untroubled it flows right across the country and then south to empty into the Caspian Sea. The Volga River brings Russia to the East, where the products of Asia can reach her by ship and caravan. Who knows? If it were not for the Volga, perhaps Russia would have stayed locked up in Europe. It is the Volga that turned the thoughts of Russians to Asia. It is the river Kama, a tributary of the Volga, that led her pioneers to Siberia, where they won an empire 4,000 miles long by 2,000 miles wide.

The Nile, the Amazon, the Yangtze are all exciting at their source. The Volga is disappointing. It doesn't leap in a waterfall, nor tumble down mountains, nor surge through canyons. Russia is a great plain—there is very little slope. In the northwest, about halfway between Moscow and the Gulf of Finland, the land is a little higher than elsewhere. This is the Valdai Plateau, and here the Volga begins.

It starts as an insignificant little spring near a village called *Volga's Source*. The spring turns into a narrow stream flowing through swamps and lakes and dried-up beds of vanished lakes. Little by little it gets wider. It picks up tributaries from both sides, bigger and bigger ones as it goes along. At the town of Gorki, where the Oka joins the Volga, both rivers are so wide that it seems as if two arms of the sea were coming together. Like our own Mississippi River, the Volga is a mile across here. But lower down, where the Kama River comes pouring in from the Ural Mountains, it is still wider.

You can't help being impressed by the vast expanse of the Volga. But the scenery along the way is rather dull, for the country is flat. There is only one place where the river gets really exciting. That is at the Samara Bend. The Volga makes a hairpin curve and cuts a deep, narrow gorge through limestone cliffs. For the rest, this is not a river of natural wonders, but a workaday river, a river that is a road to get somewhere, a highway to transport goods. It is a link that joins the forests of the north, the industry of the center and the Urals, and the rich grain fields of the Southeast.

Some distance below the hairpin curve, the River Don comes to within 45 miles of the Volga. You would think the Don had set out to be a tributary and at the last minute changed its mind. It turns west and ends up in the Sea of Azov. Meantime the Volga turns the other way and divides itself in two. Like this, as a double river, it goes on right to the Caspian Sea. There it breaks up into so many mouths that it is hard to count them. The whole enormous delta is a maze of channels and islands that keep changing their size and shape.

The delta grows and grows. Silt is making the Sea so shallow at this end that steamers coming up from the south can't come close in any more. They have to unload 40 miles offshore.

This silting up of the Caspian is a problem, but not so bad as another. The hot dry winds blowing in from the deserts of Turkestan are attacking the Caspian, too. Scientists say the Sea, which is really the world's largest lake, is drying up, shrinking at an alarming rate. In the last ten years it has become 10 feet lower, and now its surface is 85 feet below the level of the Black Sea, of which it was once a part.

Fortunately the fish that live in the Caspian don't

feel cramped for space yet. The fisheries continue to be among the world's best. Some seventy-five different kinds of fish live in the Caspian, and of them all the sturgeon is king. It is from the roe of this fish that the Russians make the famous delicacy—black caviar.

The Volga is the longest river in Europe and spreads its arms very wide. Its two biggest tributaries are each over a thousand miles long. And although the Russians have a sealed-in country, they have made the most of their mighty river. They have dug canals, joined rivers and lakes up with the Volga, and made it one continuous waterway from the Arctic Ocean and the Baltic Sea down to the Caspian.

Years ago Tsar Peter the Great built the city of St. Petersburg—which is now called Leningrad—on the Baltic Sea. He wanted his country to have a port on the western seas and thus catch up with progressive Europe. The Russians have followed the lines Peter laid down. But they haven't abandoned Asia—their great river links it with Europe. Like Leningrad, which has become a great port both of the Baltic and of the Volga, Russia faces two ways.

12 The Tartar Yoke

Mother Volga is what the Russians call their great river. But this doesn't mean that it has been theirs since ancient days. It is only 400 years since the Volga became a Russian river. How many tears and how much blood it cost before Russian boats could go freely and fearlessly down the Volga!

Look back a thousand years. See the half-savage Slavic tribes living in the upper reaches of the Dnieper River and the streams that run into it. Theirs is a cold land. It is heavily forested, the earth is hard to till. They hunt and fish for a living. They cling to the rivers because the rivers are the only roads. In the spring, when the ice breaks up, they venture out in boats they have hollowed out of tree trunks. They have furs to trade—mink and marten, beaver and squirrel and fox. They have salt to trade.

At first they exchange only with their own settlements to the south. They get barley and rye, honey, wax, and linen for their furs and their salt. Then the traders go exploring. To the north they discover a whole network of little rivers. They find that by dragging their boats a way through the marshes they can go from one stream to another. They get up to the Gulf of Finland. They venture down the Dnieper and down the Volga.

Going south they find themselves in a new kind of country. Rich black meadow land succeeds the forest. Then comes the steppe, a vast treeless plain. Here grass stretches south for hundreds of miles and eastward endlessly. Some of the grass is five, six, eight feet high.

Wandering horsemen pasture horses and cattle and sheep on the rich grass. The nomads live in round felt

Wandering horsemen on the plain lived in round felt tents.

tents. In winter they pick the tents up bodily, set them on wide wagons drawn by oxen, and go south to their winter cities. In summer they come back. These people are the Khazars. They are masters of the steppe. They have built a city at the mouth of the Volga. The Khazars welcome the traders and go up to visit their towns.

"You may use our rivers," the Khazars say, "and we will give you protection. But you must pay us tribute. We will take furs—every household must give us so many."

The Russians agree. Their boats go all the way down the Volga to the Khazar capital. They go all the way down the Dnieper to the Black Sea.

Of course, it is painful to have to pay tribute, but

Invaders drove them south, killing and plundering as they went.

the Russians don't know how lucky they are that they have to deal with the Khazars. For the wide steppe which they control has seen many much fiercer peoples and will see many more. As the centuries pass, other tribes of wandering herdsmen pour in from Asia onto the rich grasslands. The invaders drive the Khazars to the south. They kill and plunder and carry off Russian women and children. They raid the cities. They lie in wait for the merchant fleets that go down the rivers. They make the southern trade routes so unsafe that the Russians have to abandon them altogether. Hard times come. The cities depend on foreign trade, and who will venture down the river now?

But worse is in store. In Asia new tribes are stirring. The Mongols have found themselves a leader in a man they call Genghis Khan, which means Very Mighty Leader. Genghis Khan has organized his people into an army of horsemen such as the world has never seen, and he is out to conquer the world.

Part of his horde sweeps up around the Caspian Sea and comes out on the steppes. Here live the wild horsemen who have been making so much trouble for the Russians. One battle puts them to flight. Pell-mell they go across the Volga with their women and their children, their wide wagons and their tents and their herds. They don't stop till they get to the Dnieper.

"Help us," they say to the Russians. "New and strange enemies have taken our country. Tomorrow they will take yours."

The Russian princes raise an army and go to meet the Tartars, as they call the new invaders, and are terribly defeated—tens of thousands of the bravest Russians are left dead upon the field.

Panic seizes the cities. They wait trembling for the Tartars to strike. But nothing happens—as suddenly as they appeared, the Tartars disappear.

"God knows who they are or where they come from!" the Russians say.

Thirteen years pass. Then the Tartars come back.

Town after town was burned by the conquering Tartars.

Genghis Khan is dead, but his grandson, Batu, leads an army to conquer the West. Up the frozen Volga he goes and plunges into the deep Russian forests. He sends his messengers ahead.

"If you want peace," the Tartars say, "give us a tenth of your goods."

"We will give you nothing," the Russian princes answer. "When we are dead, you can have the whole."

Town after town falls. Who can stand against Batu Khan? Flames rise wherever he goes, tens of thousands of corpses lie unburied in the fields. He takes captives by the hundred thousand. Such people as escape flee to the northeast where a few Russian cities still stand.

When his conquests are done, Batu Khan sets up his headquarters on the lower Volga. He calls his town of mud brick and tents Sarai.

He arranges things very simply with the Russians. They must pay him tribute. One-tenth of their harvests, one-tenth of their flocks and horses, one-tenth of all they produce must go to Sarai. At Batu Khan's word, the Russians must furnish him as many troops as he calls for, to fight against whomsoever he desires. The princes may rule their ruined lands, but only by his permission. To get it they must travel to Sarai, kneel down before him in his tent and touch their foreheads to the ground.

"God has set a heavy yoke upon our necks," the Russians say when the Tartar tax gatherers come to get the tribute. If a householder cannot pay, his children are taken for slaves.

Body and spirit groan under the Tartar yoke. Sometimes the people rebel, and then the punishment is awful. They can have peace only by obeying the wild horsemen whom they seldom see.

For 250 years this goes on. For 250 years the people have to endure it. But at last they are strong enough to get out from under. It takes them seventy-five years more to drive the Tartars from the Volga.

In the year 1552 Tsar Ivan the Terrible moves with an immense army against the Tartar fortress Kazan, standing on the middle Volga, and takes the city. Now Tartar blood flows as Russian blood flowed. Tartar women and children are made slaves as Russian women and children were made slaves. So awful is the vengeance that the Tsar himself is moved to pity. He weeps as he beholds the bloody ruins.

But all through Russia there is rejoicing. The conquered have become the conquerors! The Volga is almost free! For centuries the Russians have been penned up in the northern forests. Soon, soon the whole great highway will be theirs.

A flood of peasants pours down the river. Some float down on rafts. Some travel over the steppes by cart caravan. They go to take possession of the rich black soil, top soil that is five feet deep and will grow the finest crops without fertilizer. The flood pours on and on down to where the green steppe fades out. It is as far as the peasants can go, for at the Volga's mouth stands another Tartar stronghold—Astrakhan.

But the power of the Tartar is nearly over. Ivan the Terrible takes the city—and the mighty river is free.

From source to mouth, the Volga flows through Russian land. Through all its length the Volga is a Russian river at last.

13 Russia's Mississippi

Perhaps you have seen a painting called "Volga Boatmen." It shows a gang of ragged, weary men toiling along the river bank towing a barge in just the same way that trackers tow junks up the Yangtze gorges. That picture is out of date. There used to be 600,000 such boatmen in Russia in the time of the tsars. Now tugboats relieve men of that fearful toil. Today the Volga is in every way a modern river— the Mississippi of the U.S.S.R.

Powerful beacons light the channel. Bulletins are issued telling the captains where the shoals are from day to day. Dredges are constantly busy somewhere, digging out silt to keep a twelve-foot depth all the way to the Caspian Sea. The docks and wharves are up-to-date, and most have modern loading and unloading devices. Indeed, in the midst of the latest model steamers and tankers and lighters and tugs, the ferries and floating refrigerators and fire-fighting ships, it seems strange to see huge rafts coming downstream, pushed by tugs. Often a raft, a quarter of a mile long and three hundred yards wide, will come downstream with nothing on it at all.

"What in the world is the meaning of that?" you wonder.

The meaning is that there are no forests in the south. The south is a treeless country. And wood is needed for all sorts of things—for building houses, for railroad ties, for pit props in mines, for machine emplacements in the factories. So the rafts are sent downriver from the forested north to be broken up at the other end.

Timber and manufactured goods are chiefly what goes down stream. Much more varied freight goes up.

All About Great Rivers of the World

As soon as the frozen river wakes from its four or five months' sleep, the busy movement begins. Tankers carry up petroleum. Barges transport metals and coal. Grain moves from the huge collective farms along the Volga. Salt from the salt desert near the Caspian goes up. Cement goes up. Fish caught both in the Volga and the sea, hides, flax, flour, machines—all these travel up the river.

In the U.S.S.R. there are 100,000 rivers. But the Volga and its tributaries get two-thirds of the freight carried on all. Besides, thousands of Volga steamers carry passengers. Some are bent on business, and some are bent on pleasure.

For the government encourages people to take a trip on the Volga. It wants them to see the progress the country has made in recent years. In the Volga region, lies half the industry of the U.S.S.R. And on the river itself are many important centers. Kazan is turning out typewriters and movie film. Gorki, the Detroit of the U.S.S.R., is making automobiles and trucks. Stalingrad, where the German army was turned back in the Second World War, is producing tractors. Astrakhan is canning fish. There are leather and fur and metal industries. At a thousand points shipbuilding is going on.

Thousands of steamers carry passengers down the Volga River.

"Spend your vacation on the Volga!" the government recommends. "See the 'Greater Volga' project realized!"

Everybody wants to see that. For the plan to reconstruct the Volga by building canals, dams, and hydroelectric stations has been the darling of all the Russian plans. The whole country has been talking about it for years.

Moscow, the capital of the U.S.S.R., stands on the Moskva River. This is a tributary of the Oka, which is a tributary of the Volga. When a canal was dug that brought the Volga itself to Moscow, there was great celebration. But when in 1952 the Volga-Don Canal opened up, the whole country spilled over with excitement.

"Moscow is now a port of five seas!" everybody repeated triumphantly.

A great dream had come true. Nobody was sorry about the labor it had cost to join the White Sea, the Baltic, the Caspian, the Black Sea, and the Sea of Azov. The country now had an inland waterway of 20,000 continuous miles. The papers pointed proudly to all the other accomplishments of the "Greater Volga" scheme. In many places the river had been so shallow that you could almost ford it. Now dams had spread water over those places so that ships could go wherever they would. Twelve hydroelectric stations stood on the Volga and 34 on its tributaries. In the Samara Bend the biggest power station in the world was being built.

"We will soon have plenty of cheap electricity for everything," the Russians said. "Electricity will even pump the Volga to irrigate our fields. We will overcome the drought that every so often ruins our crops."

Passing through their newest canal the Russians felt

as proud as we feel going through our Panama Canal.
It is thrilling to improve on Nature. Puny man seems
a giant when he can change geography.

Great dams and power stations have been built on the Volga.

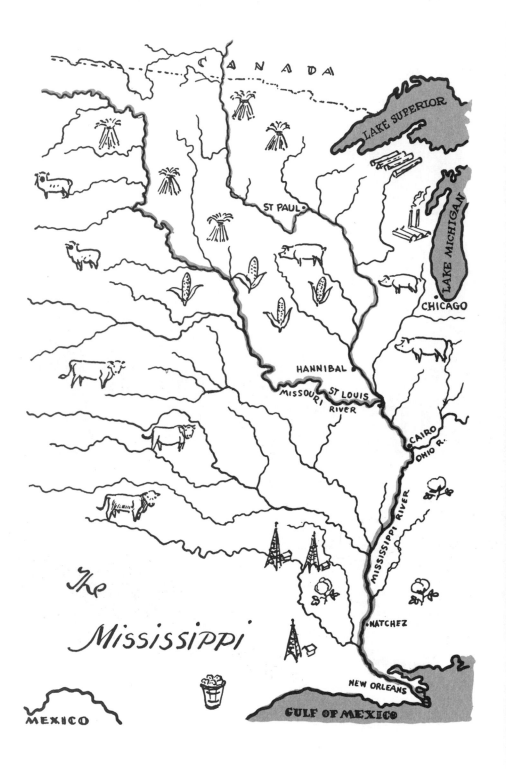

14 *Father of Waters*

On the map the Mississippi River looks like a monstrous tree. Its top reaches into Canada. Its roots are in the Gulf of Mexico. Its branches spread from the Appalachians to the Rockies. We call it the Mississippi River system, and of all our proud possessions this is the proudest.

The wonderful system drains two-fifths of our country, covering all or parts of 31 states. It gives us more than 15,000 miles of transport waterways. It takes us out into the open sea. And it has cut a valley second to none. No river system is perfect, but the Mississippi Valley seems to be the best in the world for civilized man to live in.

For a long time the river which rules this majestic valley was our western boundary. When in 1803 we bought from France the vast region lying between the Mississippi and the Rockies, it became wholly ours. But even then no one knew where its source was, not even the Chippewas, who had given it its name—Mee-zee-see-bee, Father of Waters. One explorer after another tried to find where the river began. And at last in 1832, far up in Minnesota, Henry Schoolcraft came very close to the source. It was a lake, to which he gave the name *Itasca*.

Actually the Mississippi starts five miles above Lake Itasca in a smaller lake called Little Elk. The river begins as a laughable little creek only four inches deep and so narrow that you can jump across it. At first the stream flows north, then east through lakes and over rapids as if it were heading for Lake Superior. Then it curves away in a great bow to flow at last over the Falls of St. Anthony through Minneapolis and St. Paul.

In South Dakota, the Missouri winds through steep hills.

So far the country has been mostly wild and lonely, but now the landscape changes. Fertile prairie unfolds —endless prairie, prairie as big as all of France. There are bluffs along the river and busy cities on them. And in the wide river, island after island appears. Between St. Paul and the mouth of the Missouri there are more than five hundred islands. There are so many that people seem to have run out of names and have given many of them just a number.

Powerful tributaries flow into the Mississippi. Two of them are supreme. One is the wild, yellow river we call the Missouri. It is even longer than the Mississippi, which it joins just above St. Louis. If you like, you may consider, as some do, that the Missouri and the Lower Mississippi are one. If you do that, you will make the Mississippi the second longest river in the world after the Nile. The other great tributary is the Ohio, the Beautiful River. Nearly a third of all the water which the Mississippi pours into the Gulf of Mexico comes from the Ohio.

Where it joins the Ohio, the river is very wide—a mile or more across at high water. It continues like that for half the rest of the way to the sea. Then a strange thing happens. Instead of getting wider as most rivers do, the Mississippi narrows.

The river is strange in other ways. From Cairo, Illinois, at the mouth of the Ohio on down, it curves and winds in one meander after another. Samuel Clemens, whom we know as Mark Twain, author of *Tom Sawyer* and *Huckleberry Finn*, was a steamboat pilot on the Mississippi in his youth. He knew every bend and sand bar and snag in the river and every landing and wood yard along its banks. He describes the shape of the river like this:

"If you will throw a long, pliant apple-paring over your shoulder, it will pretty fairly shape itself into an average section of the Mississippi River; that is, the nine or ten hundred miles stretching from Cairo, Illinois, southward to New Orleans, the same being wonderfully crooked, with a brief straight bit here and there at wide intervals."

The horseshoe curves, he says, are bent over so far that "if you were to get ashore at one extremity of the horseshoe and walk across the neck, half or three quarters of a mile, you could sit down and rest a couple of hours while your steamer was coming around the long elbow at a speed of ten miles an hour to take you on board again."

The Mississippi is continually trying to straighten itself out. Many a time it cuts through the narrow neck of a horseshoe curve and saves itself 25 or 35 miles at a jump. When this happens, the result is sometimes hard on a river town. Several towns have been cut off and are now a couple of miles back in the country with sand bars and forest built up in front of them.

Besides cutting off pieces of itself and turning them into crescent lakes, the river has another habit. It is constantly shifting sidewise. Islands become peninsulas; peninsulas become islands. Today a piece of land is in Louisiana, and tomorrow it is in Mississippi.

We are in the Land of Cotton here and close to the river's end. The Mississippi is a great carrier of silt.

So it is not surprising that it has built itself the world's biggest delta and keeps pushing it farther and farther out into the Gulf of Mexico. Every year the delta grows by another 250 feet or so. The great fertile mud plain is shaped like a gigantic goose's foot, and through this foot the river flows. The Mississippi breaks up into six main branches, or *passes* as they are called. Each extends far out into the water. And each has built its own little delta in front of it.

Such is the river from source to mouth. Such is the trunk of the monstrous tree.

GULF OF MEXICO

The Mississippi delta is shaped like a gigantic goose's foot.

15 "Steamboat A-Comin'!"

Behold the wide Mississippi in the days when it first became ours! It is majestic—but very lonesome. Flatboats and keelboats carry down such simple things as the pioneers have for sale—furs and corn, bear grease and venison hams, pork and lard. Upstream there is almost no traffic, for the journey is too hard. A man takes his load down, sells his craft, then walks back.

But in 1807 something happens that brings a new pace to the river—Robert Fulton's steamboat makes a trip up the Hudson. Four years later here comes a steamboat puffing down the Mississippi, and soon afterwards steamboats are making regular trips both ways. The river has suddenly come of age.

Thirty years pass. Steamers are doing a big business —these are their "flush times," before the railroads come and steal their business. But to the people along the Mississippi, steamboats have lost none of their wonder. Up in the little town of Hannibal, Missouri, Sam Clemens sees them through a boy's eyes. There are but two events in the day, he tells us. One is when a steamboat comes up from St. Louis. The other is when one comes down from Keokuk.

Hannibal drowses in the summer sun. The great Mississippi, the majestic, the magnificent Mississippi rolls its mile-wide tide along, but no one listens to the peaceful lapping of the waves against the wharf. Suddenly a Negro drayman cries out, "S-t-e-am-boat a-comin'!" and the whole dead town wakes up. Drays, carts, men, boys, all go hurrying down to the wharf. Assembled there, the people fasten their eyes on the coming boat as upon a wonder they are seeing for the first time. And the boat *is* rather a handsome sight— long and sharp and trim, with two tall, fancy-topped chimneys and a gilded device of some kind swung between them. The pilot house is all glass and "ginger-

Black smoke poured from the fancy chimneys of the old
steamboat.

bread." The paddle boxes are decorated with pictures.
The decks, fenced with clean white rails, are jammed
with passengers. Great volumes of the blackest smoke
roll and tumble out of the chimneys.

Calm, imposing, the captain stands by the big bell.
The broad landing stage is run far out over the port
bow, where a deck hand stands with a coil of rope in
his hand. Steam screams through the gauge cocks. The
captain lifts his hand, a bell rings, the wheels stop. Then
such a scramble as there is to get aboard, and to get

ashore, and to take in freight and to discharge freight, all at one and the same time! Ten minutes later the steamer is on its way, and after ten more minutes the town is dead again.

"How wonderful," thinks young Sam Clemens, the future writer, "to be a cabin boy on that steamer and come out with a white apron on and shake a tablecloth over the side where all his old comrades could see him! Better yet to be the deck hand with the coil of rope! But oh, grandest of all to be the pilot!"

This steamboat that stirs up Hannibal twice a day is just a "cheap, gaudy packet." It can't compare with the steamboats that go in for style. Some are floating palaces with cabins for 200 passengers, rich carpeting, huge mirrors, fine furniture, paintings on the doors, and a brass band playing in the lounge. The service in the big dining room is as good as in the best hotels, and the food is far better. The meals aboard the fancy steamers are famous through the country.

It is delightful to take a trip on the Mississippi if you are a cabin passenger. Many thousands of those who go up from St. Louis are not cabin passengers, however. They are people without money for luxuries. They are future Americans who have come to the Mississippi from Germany and Ireland, Norway and Sweden and Czechoslovakia. They are pioneers, seeking a home in the newly opened prairie beyond the river. They crowd the lower deck of the humbler steamers, eat such food as they have brought with them, and at night spread their bedding on the floor. The steamer will put them off at points upstream where the first roads to the unsettled West begin.

The steamboats have plenty of work to do. Besides people, they carry the products of half a continent to market, for there are as yet no railroads to the West. And when those railroads do come, there still are none that run parallel to the river. All the up-and-down transport falls on the steamers; and as speed is important, they try to cut down the time. They are forever racing one another. Far beyond the Mississippi, people take as much interest in these races as they take in the World Series today.

In June, 1870, the whole civilized world turns its eyes to the Mississippi where the steamboat *Natchez* is going to race the *Robert E. Lee* from New Orleans to St. Louis. The word is that the *Natchez* is faster and that the *Lee* hasn't a chance. But people are betting heavily; over a million dollars are in the balance.

Great crowds watched the race between the _Lee_ and _Natchez_.

Captain Cannon of the _Lee_ makes elaborate preparations for the race. He "strips" his boat. Everything that adds weight and can possibly be spared goes out. He even removes all the parts of the _Lee's_ upper works that might catch the wind and hold the boat back. He arranges with coal yards to have flatboats waiting in the middle of the river at given points so that he won't have to lose time refueling. The flatboats will be hitched onto the _Lee_ so she will keep right on going while she coals up. The captain refuses to take passengers or freight.

Captain Leathers of the _Natchez_ is too confident to make special preparations. He knows he has the better ship. He can pass the *Lee* in the first hundred miles and put her so far behind that she will never catch up.

From the time the date for the contest was set, the whole Mississippi Valley has been in a state of excitement. For weeks nobody has talked of anything but the race. And now that the afternoon of the wonderful day has come, people throng the shore.

The docks, the housetops, the vessels are crowded. Every eye is on the two competing boats, from whose chimneys thick black smoke rolls and tumbles, darkening all the air. Presently tall columns of steam burst from the escape pipes. Guns boom a farewell. A brass band plays "Hail Columbia." At five o'clock the *Robert E. Lee* backs out amid a thunder of huzzas, and five minutes later the *Natchez* leaves amid a similar burst.

The telegraph busily taps out what progress the steamboats are making. Excitement mounts, and in every village on the way people collect on the bank. At Natchez, Vicksburg, Helena, and other points it seems as if the population from miles back has turned out to greet the steamers. At Memphis ten thousand watch. All over America newspapers keep the public informed, posting bulletins to show how the race is going. The telegraph keeps ticking. As each boat passes

The steamboat *Robert E. Lee* beat the record and the *Natchez*.

Memphis, Vicksburg, and Cairo, the time of passing is cabled to Europe. For London and Paris are just as much interested as New York and Chicago.

Three days, 18 hours, and 14 minutes from the time she left New Orleans, the *Robert E. Lee* reaches the goal, beating the record as well as the *Natchez*. Thirty thousand people crowd the St. Louis wharf, the windows,

From New Orleans to St. Louis took three days and 18 hours.

and the housetops to welcome the winning steamboat. The city's businessmen tender a banquet to the captain. The wave of excitement on the Mississippi reaches an all-time high, and business stands still while people talk. The word is still that the *Natchez* is the faster boat—but Captain Cannon of the Robert E. Lee sure outsmarted Captain Leathers!

16 Men Against the Forest

"Timber-r-r!"

The lumber crew look up to see the giant crash. It is a white pine, the choicest of the trees in these Wisconsin woods—tall, straight as a mast, with branches only at the very top. There are plenty more like it. There are millions more like it in this forest of pine and spruce and tamarack that stretches hundreds of miles east and west and north all the way to Canada. The lumberjacks are dwarfed by the huge trees around them, dwarfed by the size of the forest.

Lumberjacks ran as the giant white pine crashed to the ground.

These aren't the first men to topple down the white pines of Wisconsin. The cutting started years back when settlers built homesteads on the forest's edge. Homesteaders' axes first broke the silence of these woods. The settlers felled the timber on their claims and hauled the logs to the nearest mill. The sawmills took all the men would bring, but still there wasn't enough. Along the Mississippi, towns were springing up. People were clamoring for lumber to build with— white pine, Wisconsin pine. Then crews of men went up into the woods.

These lumberjacks who have just felled the tree

belong to such a crew. They are a dozen men in all, mostly Norwegians, Swedes and Finns. They work like demons. Thirteen hours a day in weather 20 degrees below zero, they chop and trim and saw white pine. But they don't haul it to the mill. The rivers do their carrying for them. The men pile the logs up on the river bank where they wait for spring freshets to come and take them down the stream.

It's a rough life here in the lonely pinery. You wouldn't think the lumberjacks' shanty was a place for human beings. Their food is mostly bread and beans. But these are hardy fellows who can endure. They take pride in themselves because they can endure.

From dawn to dark the lumberjacks chop and lop and drag and saw, but for all that, they only chew around the edges of the forest. They cannot cut white pine enough to satisfy the growing towns. So larger crews are sent into the woods. Fifty, eighty, a hundred men attack the pines together. They cut roads deep into the forest's heart. They sprinkle the roads with water to make them icy. Teams of two, four, six horses drag huge pyramids of logs on sleds along the icy roads. Deeper and deeper into the woods marches the army of axes.

Horses drag huge pyramids of logs on sleds along icy roads.

Compared with the crews that came before, these lumberjacks live in luxury. Gone are the dark shanties where men forever had to stoop and where the wild wind came whistling through the chinks. The camps are warmly built and lighted with windows. The men sleep in bunks on mattresses filled with straw. They have fresh meat and vegetables every day. But still it's a rough, hard life. From dawn to dark the woods resound with the ring of axes, the crash of falling trees, the grating of saws, the clank of chains.

The lumberjacks are making headway. They are cutting wide swaths in the pinery. And not only in Wisconsin. All through northern Minnesota logging is going on furiously.

When spring comes and the "tote" road softens so that cutting must stop, the boldest, strongest, hardiest of the lumberjacks turn into rivermen. They wait until the ice is gone from the rivers and the water is at crest. Then with mauls and handspikes they "break" the rollways, and the whole winter's cut spills into the water with a mighty roar. It is the same on every river. In all the vast forest region the Mississippi's tributaries are carpeted with rushing logs. Down with the current they go, and down with them go the rivermen. Each holds an iron-tipped spike with which he guides and turns and drives the logs. One crew rides ahead. The men go leaping from log to log, whirling around bends, sliding down waterfalls, churning across rapids. Behind comes a second crew to pick up stranded logs and get them back into the current. Last comes the cook's raft with its little shack. The rivermen eat in shifts as the raft comes alongside. But often there isn't time for that—things are too hectic—and they snatch food out of the "nosebags" strapped on their shoulders. Sometimes they can't take time to eat at all.

Driving logs downstream is grueling work. It calls for everything a man has. Days on end the rivermen can neither sleep nor rest. Time and again they slide off

In the spring, logs are floated down the rushing, roaring river.

into the icy water—they are almost never dry. A sprained ankle is an everyday affair. Pikes are often driven into feet. Death waits at every rapid as the surging, whirling logs batter one another. Sometimes in spite of all the men can do, the logs pile up and jam. Then the whole vast carpet stands still for days, or even weeks, while the men go poking around to find the key logs that are holding up the drive. Sometimes with a single thrust of the pike pole a man can set the whole carpet rolling. Too often he pays for it with his life when the sudden rush of logs proves too much for him.

Where is the drive headed?

Some of the logs are being herded to the nearest mill. But many are destined for the great booming yards where they will be made up into rafts. For on the wide Mississippi with its busy traffic, lumber cannot go as separate logs.

At the mouth of the Chippewa River there is a famous log harbor in quiet water—Beef Slough, it is called. Booms have been set up there to hold back and enclose the logs. And what a sight it is when the yards are full! Farther than eye can reach, it is logs, logs. They are backed up for twenty miles. You would think the whole forest had floated down.

From Beef Slough rafts go down as far as St. Louis. Some are nearly a quarter of a mile long. The biggest take a crew of 35 raftsmen, all hardy fellows with adventure in their blood. For it's no pleasure trip down to St. Louis. Summer storms lash the raft. Low water strands it. Fierce rapids wait to hurl it to destruction.

But the rafts get through. Year after year the great rafts come down. It seems as if there is no end to the white pine forests of the north. But it only seems that way. In 1883 the last raft from the Wisconsin pineries comes down the Mississippi. The army of axes has nearly finished its work on the Wisconsin giants. It is busy now in Minnesota, where there is still white pine to cut. In 1912 forty thousand lumberjacks go up into the Minnesota logging camps.

But the story of lumber on the Mississippi is almost over. The white pine is vanishing fast. Another few years and the camps are empty. The sawmills are shut down. Grass grows in the streets of sawmill towns. The ring of the ax, the crash of falling trees, the grind of saws, the clank of chains are heard no more.

Silence reigns again in the desolation that was once a forest.

Only stumps remain of gorgeous white pine forests.

17 Flood!

In 1927 there was disaster in the Mississippi Valley from Cairo, Illinois, to the Gulf of Mexico. In all our peacetime history there had never been such great disaster. The Mississippi overflowed and took 13,000,000 acres of land for its own. Four hundred lives were lost. Seven hundred thousand people were made homeless. There was property damage amounting to $350,000,-000.

Why did it happen? Why did Ol' Man River go wild?

Floods in the valley are nothing new. Since ancient days the Mississippi has overflowed its banks. We know that is true because at the edges where the over-flow stopped, it kept depositing layer upon layer of silt till it had built up low embankments on either side. There were times when the Mississippi was extra full. Then it would spill over these natural levees which it had built. But then no harm was done because no one lived there. This was swamp land that belonged to the river. The Indians had no need of it.

Then the white men came. As soon as they had built New Orleans, they began to hem the river in. They built dikes along the river front to keep the Mississippi out of their town. As planters took up claims along the river, they, too, built levees. Or, rather, they raised the natural levees higher. That didn't bother Ol' Man River very much. The planters were few. There were wide gaps between one piece of levee and another. The river could flow through the gaps—they were natural spill-ways.

Time passed. Towns and villages sprang up all the way from Cairo to the Gulf. Farms filled in the spaces between. The levees grew and grew, longer and longer. At last they lined the river on each side for a thousand miles—from the Gulf to the mouth of the Ohio.

Most of the swamps beyond the levees—the swamps that had belonged to the river—were drained now. They had been turned into farm land. People didn't want the Mississippi to take back their rich farm land. So they kept building the levees higher. They learned how to make them stronger, too. They wove enormous mattresses of willow branches and set them against the river side of the levees to keep the earth from washing away.

But Ol' Man River found the weak places and broke through. All through the 1880s the Mississippi kept breaking through. Then in 1903 and 1907, in 1913 and 1922 it broke through even stronger and higher levees.

And all the time the floods were getting worse. People couldn't understand why. But the reasons were plain to see.

One was that by shutting the river in, we had caused the water to run faster, and that had made it more destructive. We had "filed the teeth and ground the claws of the tiger."

But there was another reason. More water was pouring into the rivers. We had cut down the forests and left the hillsides bare. For not content with taking the white pine for building our thousand cities and towns, we had gone back and cut down cedar for fence posts, tamarack for railroad ties, spruce for paper pulp. We had left the forests stripped. Then raging fires had swept over the ravaged woodland, leaving the ground without a cover. There was no network of tree roots to soak up the rain and hold it in the soil. There were no trees or bushes to break the fall of the raindrops and make them sink gently into the earth. The heavy rains rushed in torrents down the cut and burned-over hillsides and poured into the streams.

In the South we had chopped down the trees, plowed up the land, and made cotton king. We had run the furrows up and down instead of around the slopes. In winter we had left the earth without a cover. Then the rains had swept over, cutting deep gullies and running off.

There had always been floods, but now they were getting worse; and in 1927, after a season of heavy rains, came the worst flood of all. All the way from Cairo to Natchez the levees tumbled. Western Mississippi was a sea. Northern Louisiana was a sea. New

Even steel bridges were swept away in the Mississippi flood.

Orleans was saved only by dynamiting the levee below the city. An endless waste of yellow water poured over the towns and villages and farms. Steel bridges were swept away. Railroads were abandoned. Mills and sugar refineries were ruined. White-pillared plantation houses stood in water halfway up to their roofs.

On the broken levees refugees by the thousand sat with whatever animals and household goods they had been able to save. Bewildered families looked mutely out upon the raging sea. Once their homes had stood there. Now only chimneys and the tops of trees poked out above the water. And on the surface floated dead

Homes were abandoned; men and animals sought shelter.

animals, trees, trash, fences, bridges, boxcars, houses, barns, chicken coops. The drift from 54 flooded tributaries added itself to all the local drift.

Crawling out of the water, wild animals shared the broken levees with man. Deer, rabbits, foxes had lost their fear of him and of his dogs. Wild turkeys and quail sat on the piled-up furniture. Children made friends with muskrats. Every creature was welcomed— only the snake was denied a refuge.

Sea planes of the Navy roared over the flooded countryside to spot people clinging to roof tops and trees. Steamers and boats moved around over what had

been dry land. They picked up the stranded and homeless and took them to Red Cross camps. They rescued
animals, too. Near Natchez 15,000 head of cattle had
to be saved from the levees, mounds, and ridges where
they had been stranded. Some were so hungry that they
had eaten all the bark off trees as high as they could
reach.

All America answered the valley's call for help. The
Red Cross asked for $5,000,000. Then it asked for
$10,000,000 more. The money poured in. Food and
clothing poured in. The railroads handled them without
charge.

When months afterwards the Mississippi returned to
its channel and the people went back to scrape the slime
from their homes, they were much sadder and wiser
folk. They were convinced at last that levees alone
could never hold back the mighty Mississippi. A river
that carried every drop of water flowing down two-
thirds of the continent couldn't be kept behind walls.
Man would have to give back to the Mississippi what he
had taken from it—its spillways.

Committees were already working out a plan. The
levees must be rebuilt, but in a new way, they said. If
the river was bound to break through anyway, at least

When flood waters subsided, farmers found their land in ruins.

people could decide where the breaks should come. Here and there in unimportant places where farms and villages were few, stretches of levee must be purposely left weak. Then when the river got dangerously high, it could break through into the lowlands at these unimportant places.

This wasn't all the committees said. They said that

flood control of the mighty Mississippi meant flood control of the tributaries, too. And that meant control of the little rivers that emptied into them, the little rivers 'way back in the mountains.

"We must build dams there," they said, "to hold back the water and let it through in the dry spells. And at the same time we could use the water to make electricity for the nearby farms and towns. We can stop the floods. And if we do it the right way, we will do much more. We will make the whole Mississippi Valley over. We took it apart. We can put it together again."

One thing the experts insisted on—steps must be taken to save the valley's topsoil. For every year, they said, the Mississippi was taking toll of the land, more terrible than any the river took in flood time.

"Spring and fall the water comes down from a thousand hillsides," the soil experts said. "It is washing the top off the valley. We cut down the forests without any thought of the future. We plowed up land and planted cotton and moved west when the land wore out. Now every year 400,000,000 tons of topsoil, our most valuable natural resource, are being washed into the Gulf of Mexico. One-twentieth of the valley is ruined for agriculture forever. One-fourth of the topsoil of the entire valley has been carried into the Gulf. We must plant trees on the hillsides and worn-out fields. We must teach the farmers the right way to plow."

America had had a terrible experience. It was willing to listen—and to act.

Channels were dredged in the river and spillways were built.

18 A King Without Glamor

We have learned that it is easier to destroy than to create, quicker to chop down and waste than grow and build. It will take us a very long time to repair all the damage we have done to the Valley. But Ol' Man River is pretty well tamed. The Federal Government itself has taken charge of the Mississippi, and there is every hope it won't go on a rampage again.

Sam Clemens would hardly know the river today. Government engineers have dredged the channel to

keep a nine-foot depth all the way. They have short-
ened the river many miles. They have built dams and
locks and dikes. They have seen to it that levees are
protected by the very best of mattresses. Some are made
of slabs of concrete and steel rods. Some are of heavy
metal cable and steel mesh inside a blanket of asphalt
paving. It is hard to believe the river could break
through such defenses.

To keep the Mississippi fit for commerce and rolling
where it belongs is no easy job. Engineers are forever
busy with concrete and wood, with asphalt and steel,
with dredges and derricks. The river is still restless—it
keeps piling up silt here and taking it away there.
Sometimes in a single month a bar will shift a mile. So
motorboats scud around taking soundings, changing
markers, checking lights.

And what of the traffic on this modernized, well-
groomed river?

It is a traffic of barges, not steamboats; of freight, not
passengers.

That sounds workaday, and so it is. Still, it is quite
a sight to see a big barge tow coming along, maybe 24
steel barges with a single square-nosed tug pushing the
whole lot. Just as there are different kinds of cars in

A square-nosed tug may push as many as twenty-four barges.

a freight train—boxcars and flatcars, tankers and gondolas—so there are different kinds of barges in a barge train. Each is suited to its special cargo. Open barges, covered barges, tank barges and hopper barges may all go along together with their tugboat for an engine.

It's a slow train. It makes at best six miles an hour going downstream. Upstream it averages three. A tow voyage takes weeks—so naturally things that will spoil can't travel this way. The goods that go up and down the river are bulky, heavy freight that can take its time getting places. Oil is the leader. All the oil it takes to heat Minneapolis and St. Paul comes up the river. Gasoline for Pittsburgh and Chicago and the Twin Cities

At best the barge makes only six miles an hour downstream.

goes up. Sulfur for Buffalo's steel mills is second only to oil and gas. The coal from which Chicago makes its light and power is river-borne. Steel, ores, sand and gravel, lumber and fertilizer, cement and paper, grain and soybeans and rice, sugar and molasses—these are the things that travel on the river.

A barge tow is slow, but it gets a mountain of goods from one place to another. For a single barge carries as much as a whole long freight train. One tow delivered enough pipe to lay forty miles of pipeline. Another took down more than a quarter of a million bushels of grain. Still another carried as much sand and gravel as would have filled 165 railroad cars.

All About Great Rivers of the World

A hundred million tons of freight and more move on the river every year. And who is the unsung hero of this vast operation?

It is the towboat pilot. For no matter how hard the engineers work to smooth his path, it is still a difficult one. He has to remember the shape of the river, has to remember every bend, island, and sand bar. He has to watch the wind and "read" the water. He has to make the decisions. How shall the barges be arranged so that they make the bends all right? How close shall he shave the bank? How near shall he skirt the sand bar? Shall he risk thousands of dollars by pushing ahead in a fog? He worries from the time he leaves home port to the time he gets back weeks later.

But you would never know it to see him. There he sits in the pilot house, dressed in his grimy pants and sport shirt. He doesn't have a wheel. He presses levers to steer the tow. And he does it as if it were the easiest thing in the world to bring a thousand feet of barges around a sharp bend. As he passes a town where a railway train is standing, he toots his whistle just for fun. There's a lot of rivalry between the railways and the barges.

The pilot is king of the barge tow, but he is a very informal king, a king without glamor. He takes his job casually, as it comes, he makes his decisions, he gets through. And the towns take him casually. When he pulls up at a dock, the whole population doesn't rush down pell-mell as it did to the cry of "Steamboat a-comin'!" That excitement is gone as surely as the excitement that stirred the country when the *Natchez* raced the *Robert E. Lee.*

But that's not to say things are dull on the river. There's a sense of a big job being done with a minimum of strain and fuss. There's a sense of power and control on the river. The Mississippi is in tune with the twentieth century. It is geared to the Industrial Age.

The modern towboat pilot steers the tow by pressing levers.

Index

Index

Index

SPACE SCIENCE

All About Satellites and Space Ships
by David Dietz
All About Rockets and Space Flight
by Harold D. Goodwin
All About the Planets
by Patricia Lauber
All About the Stars
by Anne Terry White

PHYSICAL SCIENCE

All About the Atom
by Ira M. Freeman
All About Electricity
by Ira M. Freeman
All About Radio and Television
by Jack Gould
All About Engines and Power
by Sam and Beryl Epstein
All About the Wonders of Chemistry
by Ira M. Freeman
All About Sound and Ultrasonics
by Ira M. Freeman

NATURAL SCIENCE

All About Animals and Their Young
by Robert M. McClung
All About Horses
by Marguerite Henry
All About Dogs
by Carl Burger
All About Monkeys
by Robert S. Lemmon
All About Whales
by Roy Chapman Andrews
All About Fish
by Carl Burger
All About Birds
by Robert S. Lemmon
All About the Insect World
by Ferdinand C. Lane
All About Moths and Butterflies
by Robert S. Lemmon
All About Snakes
by Bessie M. Hecht
All About Dinosaurs
by Roy Chapman Andrews
All About Strange Beasts of the Past
by Roy Chapman Andrews
All About Strange Beasts of the Present
by Robert S. Lemmon
All About the Flowering World
by Ferdinand C. Lane

EARTH SCIENCE

All About the Planet Earth
by Patricia Lauber
All About Mountains and Mountaineering
by Anne Terry White
All About Volcanoes and Earthquakes
by Frederick H. Pough
All About Rocks and Minerals
by Anne Terry White
All About the Ice Age
by Patricia Lauber
All About the Weather
by Ivan Ray Tannehill
All About the Sea
by Ferdinand C. Lane
All About Sailing the Seven Seas
by Ruth Brindze
All About Undersea Exploration
by Ruth Brindze
All About Great Rivers of the World
by Anne Terry White
All About the Jungle
by Armstrong Sperry
All About the Desert
by Sam and Beryl Epstein
All About the Arctic and Antarctic
by Armstrong Sperry

PHYSIOLOGY AND MEDICINE

All About the Human Body
by Bernard Glemser
All About Great Medical Discoveries
by David Dietz

GREAT DISCOVERIES

All About Archaeology
by Anne Terry White
All About Prehistoric Cave Men
by Sam and Beryl Epstein
All About Famous Scientific Expeditions
by Raymond P. Holden
**All About Famous Inventors
and Their Inventions**
by Fletcher Pratt

THE UNITED STATES

All About Our 50 States
by Margaret Ronan
All About the U.S. Navy
by Edmund L. Castillo

MUSIC

All About the Symphony Orchestra
by Dorothy Berliner Commins

551.4
WH1   **White, Anne Terry**

              All about great
              rivers of the
              world

DATE DUE
